RECREATING THE PAST

Dedication:

To Tim Taylor for making it all happen

Recreating the Past

Victor Ambrus & Mick Aston

First published 2001

PUBLISHED IN THE UNITED KINGDOM BY:

Tempus Publishing Ltd
The Mill, Brimscombe Port
Stroud, Gloucestershire GL5 2QG

PUBLISHED IN THE UNITED STATES OF AMERICA BY:

Arcadia Publishing Inc.
A division of Tempus Publishing Inc.
2 Cumberland Street
Charleston, SC 29401
1-888-313-2665

Tempus books are available in France, Germany and Belgium
from the following addresses:

Tempus Publishing Group	Tempus Publishing Group	Tempus Publishing Group
21 Avenue de la République	Gustav-Adolf-Straße 3	Place de L'Alma 4/5
37300 Joué-lès-Tours	99084 Erfurt	1200 Brussels
FRANCE	GERMANY	BELGIUM

British Library Cataloguing in Publication Data.
A catalogue record for this book is available from the British Library.

ISBN 0 7524 1909 9

Typesetting and origination by Tempus Publishing.
PRINTED AND BOUND IN GREAT BRITAIN

Contents

Acknowledgements

We have been encouraged and helped by a lot of people, including many from the *Time Team* programmes. Tim Taylor, the producer of the programmes, gave his blessing to the project; it is a pleasure for us to dedicate the book to him. Many of the participants have also been very generous with their time and assistance.

We would like to thank in particular Sue Francis and Steve Breeze of Creative TV for earlier work on some of the graphics used here. Also Professor Margaret Cox for advice on the pathology for some of the incidents depicted here, and Stuart Ainsworth on the landscape analysis which provided the background for some of the pictures. Steve Minnitt of *Somerset County Council County Museum* kindly allowed us to use the Forestier reconstruction of the Glastonbury Lake Village.

Teresa Hall has helped greatly with text preparation, editing, locating illustrations and compiling the index. It is again a pleasure to acknowledge all at Tempus for their encouragement during production — Peter Kemmis Betty, Della Cantillion and Anne Phipps.

1 Introduction

This book is about archaeological reconstruction drawings — that is a modern artist's attempts to depict scenes from the past, almost as if he was there, looking over a particular scene in the countryside or in a town.

Why do we need to do this, what information is at hand to help us and how accurate can we make such drawings and paintings — can they ever be like it *actually* was in the past?

Generally speaking the further we go back the more difficult it is to get the evidence to reconstruct any accurate version of the past, and what it was like to live then becomes more difficult for us to fathom out. This is certainly true for the Palaeolithic and Mesolithic periods of the stone age, less so for the Neolithic and Bronze Ages. For the Iron Age the evidence is better and it is rather good for the Roman period. The Dark Ages and early Saxon periods are still very difficult while for the Medieval period there is a lot of information. After 1600 there is an increasing volume of evidence of all types to help us.

In order to attempt any pictorial reconstruction of life in earlier times we are totally dependent on the evidence that we can assemble from various investigative activities. For most of the time-span back to when people began permanently to occupy the British Isles after the last glaciation (say around 13,000 BC) and for any time before then when people visited Britain in interglacial periods, archaeology is our principal means of getting evidence. This not only includes excavation, which is what most people think archaeologists do, but other techniques such as field survey, aerial reconnaissance, geophysical surveys and environmental sampling.

For the historical period, roughly from the Anglo-Saxons onwards (though there is a 'history' for the latest prehistoric decades and the Roman period), there are records and documents which give us additional, if different, complementary information. These can of course help enormously when attempting any reconstruction.

For the earlier prehistoric periods environmental archaeology provides just the sort of evidence to enable an artist to fill in the details of the landscape and surroundings of the site under

2

2 *The medieval countryside — a settlement at Waddon in Dorset with houses, crofts (farmyards) and surrounding fields*

investigation. These relatively new techniques, which include pollen and snail analysis for example, mean that we can say whether an area was open or wooded, grassland or scrub at any particular time, with considerable confidence.

What are we trying to show in these reconstructions? Often a general view, usually an air view, of a scene with buildings, fields, roads and so on, is what is produced. From this we can see the site under investigation in its former setting, with the appropriate buildings, defences, and roads alongside the natural features of hills, valleys, floodplains, rivers and streams. Fields with crops, animals and natural vegetation of woodland, marshes, fens or scrub can be added. Little can be seen of the detail of people, their dress, and activities for earlier periods — but then we often do not know much about this in detail.

Rather less common are close-up views where we are in among the people of a time, engaged in their activities and able to see them, their dress, adornments of jewellery, weapons and equipment at close hand. This reflects the sort of evidence archaeology can retrieve — it is good at plans of buildings and settlement layouts, not quite so good at reconstructing day-to-day activities — particularly if it is of a non-functional, non-practical aspect where little in the way of physical traces are left behind.

The history of archaeological reconstruction drawing is not particularly long, being mostly confined to the twentieth century, and to a large extent it has affected the development of archaeology itself. The paintings of Ancient Britons by John White from the end of the sixteenth century are an exception in being so early but they mark the beginning of an interest in the past, in that case as the result of meeting native Americans.

It is perhaps a surprise to find that the idea of reconstructing a site or building on paper is

3

A body being cremated on a pyre of wood (above)
Cremation and funeral procession at the gatehouse of Birdoswald Fort with a typical civil settlement (vicus) outside (below)

4

9

5

Glastonbury Lake Village by Forestier (1911). An early attempt at an archaeological reconstruction — in this case of the settlement of round houses with a jetty

relatively new one. Up to around 1900 there do not appear to be any attempts to take an archaeological site or a ruined castle or abbey and show what it might have been like in its heyday drawing on the artist's imagination. There were Victorian paintings depicting the past — such as William Bell Scott's showing 'King Egfrid persuading Cuthbert to forsake his hermitage on Farne and become a bishop' (1856, Watlington Hall, Morpeth) or William Hole's (1846-1917) 'Mission of St Columba to the Picts' (Scottish National Portrait Gallery) — but these always showed a particular *event* in a romantic and imaginary setting and sometimes with the objects shown being from totally different periods!

It is a surprise that General Pitt Rivers, regarded by many as the father of modern British archaeology, did not commission drawings or paintings of the sites he excavated in the late nineteenth century so that he could show people what he thought they looked like. He had models made of the sites he excavated and a museum built so that people could see the finds, he was clearly interested in some aspects of public education about archaeology but it did not extend to the idea of artistic reconstructions.

Some of the earliest reconstructions were executed by A. Forestier following the discovery of the Glastonbury Lake Village at the end of the nineteenth century. One shows a bird's-eye view of the settlement, others show close views of gambling, grinding corn and metal-working taking place (Coles and Minnitt 1995), while my favourite (**5**) is a grand view approaching the settlement by canoe and being met by an awesome chieftain (dated 1911). The *Illustrated London News* commissioned the pictures as they had for other sites and continued to do so on into the early twentieth century.

However, the best-known and perhaps the most influential of all artists who have attempted archaeological reconstructions is Alan Sorrell (1904-74) whose drawings and paintings of so many sites dominated the mid-twentieth century. It is perhaps no exaggeration to say that our view of the past, or at least many, many aspects of it, is conditioned and coloured by the drawings of this one man. Site after site owned by (what is now) English Heritage, Cadw — Welsh Historic Monuments and Historic Scotland were painted by Sorrell, and many of the important excavations of the century were also depicted such as Sutton Hoo, Baginton, Lullingstone, Cheddar, Jarlshof and Wharram Percy.

Most of his views are either air or bird's-eye views. There are few ground-level views and not many with close-ups of people engaged in various activities. The atmosphere is often overpowering in these reconstructions with glowering clouds, threatening rain and squally wind giving the impression of imminent disaster. Once asked by Brian Hobley, when Sorrell was working at the Lunt Roman Fort at Baginton, Coventry, why this was, Sorrell is reported to have replied, 'life is like that'. Nevertheless, the draughtsmanship and attention to detail is impressive and the reconstructions are real works of art.

Sorrell worked closely with archaeologists familiar with the site of which he was to produce a reconstruction drawing. Discussion at each stage resulted in modifications as details of building size, shape, roof and walling came to light (see for example the drawings of Sorrell (1981, 19) and several in Humphreys (1980)). The same still goes on of course. Brian Davison describes the process between a reconstruction artist and a group of specialist researchers — 'reconstructing the past on paper is a very collaborative venture' (Davison 1997, 62-3).

This is the way Victor and I have worked on the many sites we have visited. Often Victor does some rough sketches from a particular viewpoint (**6**) which we then discuss, criticise, alter and amend (**1**) before a more satisfactory version is produced. Details of the layout of the landscape are obtained from air photographs or high views over the site and incorporated along with any environmental evidence which suggests river courses, tree cover and other vegetation.

7

Celtic cavalry in late Roman armour attacking the invading Saxons. This was a re-enactment by brilliant horsemen giving a demonstration on Chatham Common. It was a bitterly cold day but I enjoyed drawing the action — V

The York 'Shambles' as they may have looked in the Middle Ages. A lot of shouting crowds and funny smells — V

8

The baton has passed from Sorrell in recent decades to a new group of artists. Notable among these are Terry Ball, Jane Brayne, Peter Connolly, Judith Dobie, Peter Dunn, Peter Froste, Frank Gardiner, and Ivan Lapper. Much of their work is like that of Alan Sorrell (though with better weather) but there are more close-ups of people and grand views. Some, like the work of Chris Jones-Jenkins, is concerned almost entirely with getting the architectural reconstructions correct for castles and abbeys.

Into this tradition fits the work of Victor Ambrus. He has illustrated over 300 books including many children's books. However his work is best known for historical subjects and classical literature illustrations for Oxford University Press as well as the sites excavated by *Time Team* for Channel 4's well-known series. To date, 80 programmes have been made with Victor producing one or more illustrations for each programme.

This book is not about *Time Team*, since it has formed only a small part of Victor's output, but most of the illustrations are from the series, where the two authors met and have enjoyed a fruitful collaboration.

How does an artist set about producing an archaeological reconstruction? How is the view chosen, season, time of day, relevant activities to be depicted and so on? When and why is colour chosen rather than black and white? What are the problems encountered and how are these mastered to produce the finished piece of work?

9

How it all happens — in Victor's own words

My work starts by looking at the site and the landscape, and doing some research work even before my pencil touches the paper. Most of the time any drawing, or painting, has to be done very quickly, because most archaeological digs that I work on take only three days. The drawing can be very enjoyable if the sun shines and I can find a comfortable viewpoint — or can be absolutely horrible, with sheets of rain and wind coming down on you from all angles.

There is also the question of what to draw on — I am only armed with a folder, a lightweight drawing board which has seen better days, and strong white card (but no chair or tables), so I have to find what I can to work on.

Drawings are always done in pencil because they change almost continuously! This can be to do with new discoveries, like new walls, or often the experts changing their minds. A building starting as two-storey could easily end up as one storey only, because the walls discovered could only support one floor.

A lot of my time is spent picking archaeological brains, chasing after them around the trenches and pestering them for the latest information. By the end of the first day I usually have a mental picture of what is happening on the site — but not the details.

Mick and I then have one of our 'chats', as he calls it, which is in fact a very important exchange of ideas and sketches of what we may have on the site. Buildings, forts and landscapes then gradually emerge onto the paper and take shape. The eraser is always to hand as the drawing will evolve and change as the archaeology is progressing. On the last day — latest and final evidence on hand — two or three more drawings will be finalised, buildings with people, haystacks, dogs and rubbish tips included.

People are important to me — after all there would be no buildings, artefacts or settlements without them. I love drawing reconstructions of what people looked like, what they did, what they wore, how they behaved. Grinding up corn, riding horses, cremating and burying relatives, throwing pots; all fascinating subjects. Sometimes we have 're-enactors', groups of wonderful enthusiasts who make their own totally authentic clothes, be they twelfth-century or Cromwellian — and give me a unique insight into what people wore, what thay ate and how they fought. I always try to get some drawings of them and you will find a few in the book.

Reconstructions from skeletons that we find are also very exciting. I work very closely with pathologists — usually with Professor Margaret Cox — and from bones and skulls we work out what the dead person looked like. This is generally done in the form of a drawing, but recently I went three-dimensional and made a clay reconstruction of a male leper's skull in all its gory detail. Even I found it repulsive, but it was a fascinating experiment (figure **112**).

Occasionally all the work is done in colour, such as the prehistoric landscape at Elveden, where the weather was wonderful, or in York on a multi-period excavation where I produced three separate watercolours on Viking, Roman and early Middle Ages reconstructions.

I normally live a quiet life illustrating Chaucer, Dickens and Shakespeare, broken by hectic days of exciting digs with *Time Team* where we are all one big happy family, facing yet another archaeological puzzle, be it Roman villas or Norman Castles.

Bringing it all alive is my aim. As a background to archaeology I include some of my full-colour historical illustrations from the Battle of Hastings to Waterloo. Warfare on horseback is one of my favourite subjects. I once went to the extreme of taking a sabre on horseback to practice cuts on pine trees. After nearly beheading a poor mushroom picker I gave this up. You can take research a little too far!

10

As our understanding of the past improves and our views of it become clearer the role of the reconstruction artist is vital in helping to picture places and events as they might have been. Their work is pivotal and of great importance in encouraging archaeologists to interpret their evidence.

Thinking of how we might reconstruct a site under excavation (either physically, as a three-dimensional model, or on paper) should affect how it is excavated and what questions are asked of the site — and indeed, generate new questions when it is *not* clear what a site might have looked like. There is therefore a real feedback mechanism once the concept of archaeological reconstruction is undertaken. Apart from giving the public, and especially children, an idea of what a place might have looked like, this is one of the most important aspects of reconstruction drawing.

We can probably never fully understand and envisage what life was really like in earlier times, but what understanding we have is in no small measure due to the archaeological reconstructions made by such artists. Because of this we owe them a great debt; we should encourage more attempts at depicting aspects of earlier lives and recreating the past.

References

There is not a huge amount of literature about archaeological reconstruction drawing — the best references are the drawings themselves contained in textbooks (often for children) and site reports and museum displays. The following is a brief selection.

John Coles and Stephen Minnitt, 1995, *Industrious and Fairly Civilized: The Glastonbury Lake Village*. Somerset Levels Project and Somerset County Council

Brian Davison, 1997, *Picturing the Past: Through the Eyes of Reconstruction Artists*. English Heritage Gatekeeper Series, Cadw

Paul Hulton, 1984, *America 1585: The Complete Drawings of John White*. British Museum, London

Peter Humphries, 1980, *Alan Sorrell: Early Wales Recreated*. National Museum of Wales, Cardiff. With a list of published works by Alan Sorrell

Mark Sorrell (ed), 1981, *Alan Sorrell: Reconstructing the Past*. Batsford, London

Time Chart

Modern	2000
	1750
Post-Medieval	
	1540
Medieval	
	1066
Early Medieval	
	410
Roman	
	AD 43
Iron Age	
	*c.*600 BC
Bronze Age	
	2000 BC
Neolithic	
	4000 BC
Mesolithic	
	8000 BC
Palaeolithic	

2 Prehistory

The Palaeolithic

The Palaeolithic (or Old Stone Age) is a very difficult period to deal with. Little in the way of sites and settlements remain (many of these are in caves which have been poorly excavated in the past) and the material culture is dominated by stone implements and a few bone objects. Virtually nothing remains of the wood, skin, horn and other materials which must have been used.

This is a period before agriculture when hunting, fishing and gathering wild foods provided the normal subsistence and the source of many raw materials in use at the time. So any reconstructions will assume hunting strategies, dress skins and furs, and the use of stone tools.

Illustrated here are three sites — Elveden in Suffolk dating to approximately 400,000 BC, Stanton Harcourt around 200,000 BC and Cheddar in Somerset around 11,000 BC.

Finds of tools and occupation sites, perhaps indicated by fires and tool-making debris, are very rare on archaeological excavations. After all, this period of occupation is very long (hundreds of thousands of years), a very long time ago, and there were few people with little impact on their surroundings. It is not surprising that little trace is left behind.

Though we often only get little indication of people on such sites, there is a lot more we can find out. Over the vast length of time of the Palaeolithic there were a succession of glaciations, and warmer interglacial periods when the climate might be like today or even slightly warmer. Using a battery of environmental archaeological techniques we can make a good attempt at reconstructing the landscape and scenery of the time with the animals and plants which were around when prehistoric hunter groups passed through. Two of the examples shown here demonstrate this clearly.

Elveden — straight tusked elephant

11

12

(left) Elveden — reconstruction painting of the river which ran through the site with contemporary plants, animals and visiting humans, who left their tools behind.

A landscape that had changed a lot, the river bed is still there but the river is long gone.

I had a lovely sunny day to paint this — V

(right) Elephant, Stanton Harcourt

13

(right) Bear, Stanton Harcourt

14

15

Stanton Harcourt, general view (below) showing an early course of the River Thames with grazing bison and mammoths

16

Figure **12** is a view of the river at Elveden, Suffolk, with palaeolithic hunters stalking straight-tusked elephants while others prepare blades and tools. The size of the river and the immediate scenery are based on excavation by Nick Ashton of the British Museum. The animals represented (such as the picture top left) are based on the evidence from this site and elsewhere and what is generally understood from this period. People are known from the flint implements found and tool preparation from the debris left behind and excavated by archaeologists.

This is a landscape that has changed totally in the last nearly half a million years. The original pattern of rivers and streams ran in a completely different direction to the modern drainage system and this earlier landscape is buried several metres down. It has only been seen in clay pits when prehistoric tools and old land surfaces have been recognized.

Evidence for all of the plant and

Mammoths in the river, Stanton Harcourt

17

This reconstruction was based on dramatic evidence. A young mammoth calf was trapped amongst driftwood and the mother tried to rescue it. In the log jam they both perished, we found the two remains together entangled in branches — V

animal species shown in the foreground has been found from environmental research on the site.

The second site, at Stanton Harcourt, is only half the age of Elveden but that still dates from 200,000 years ago! Here, in a similar fashion, we know that people were about — hand-axes have been found but little else. Like Elveden, the remains of the earlier landscape are several metres down and have been located, in this case over a much wider area, because of large scale gravel extraction.

Remains of mammoth, elephant, bear, lion, hyena, bison and horse were present together with fishbones and remains of insects and beetles (**13**, **14** and **15**). Across the landscape ran a large river channel, part of a system of abraded river courses with sand banks and islands between. These were surrounded by marshes and swamps (**16**). Animals got stuck in the mud and fast flowing parts of the river; others died and disintegrated, their bones collecting in tangles of wood and vegetation (**17**).

Cheddar Gorge is one of the best places in the country to see evidence of people in the later Palaeolithic period. In the limestone are numerous caves, which have produced masses of evidence of occupation with thousands of flint implements, bone tools and objects.

Overleaf is the rock shelter at Cooper's Hole with a group of hunters beside a fire figure **18**, while **20** is a hunt in progress. Problems of reconstruction here include depiction of any ancillary structures such as windbreaks, tents or shelters by the cave, clothing, if any, evidence of body decoration, necklaces and so on. Although it is difficult to make too close a comparison with recent and modern hunter-gatherer groups in the world, study of these can of course help us to see the equipment and lifestyle of an early hunter-gatherer group.

18

Cheddar — Coopers Hole Cave in the side of Cheddar Gorge and how it might have looked in the Palaeolithic period

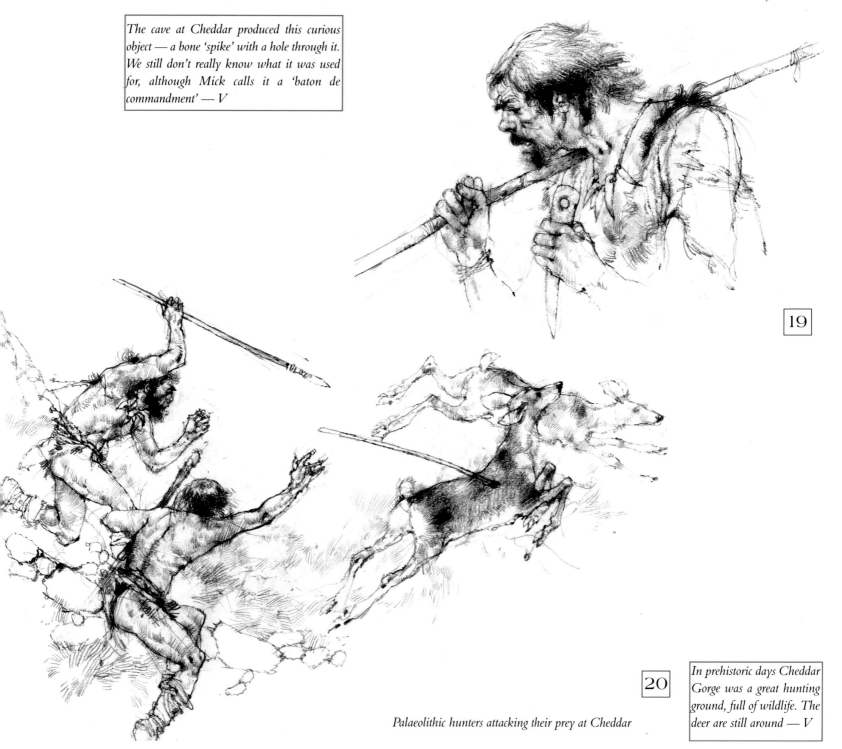

The cave at Cheddar produced this curious object — a bone 'spike' with a hole through it. We still don't really know what it was used for, although Mick calls it a 'baton de commandment' — V

19

20

Palaeolithic hunters attacking their prey at Cheddar

In prehistoric days Cheddar Gorge was a great hunting ground, full of wildlife. The deer are still around — V

The reconstruction artist must inevitably rely to some extent on images of these modern groups, albeit in a different climatic and vegetation setting. From around 40,000 BC we are dealing with 'modern' people, so they should look like us, if less well-groomed, younger and better built!

Figure **19** on the previous page shows an implement sometimes found on palaeolithic sites — the 'baton de commandment', a bone with a hole carved in the end. The name implies early antiquaries thought it was a badge or symbol of rank, but it might have a more prosaic function as a shaft-straightener for arrows as the hole frequently has grooves in it.

At Cheddar (**21**) there is interesting possible evidence of cannibalism. Bones including a skull (**22**) have been found with cut marks made by flint implements suggesting skin and flesh were

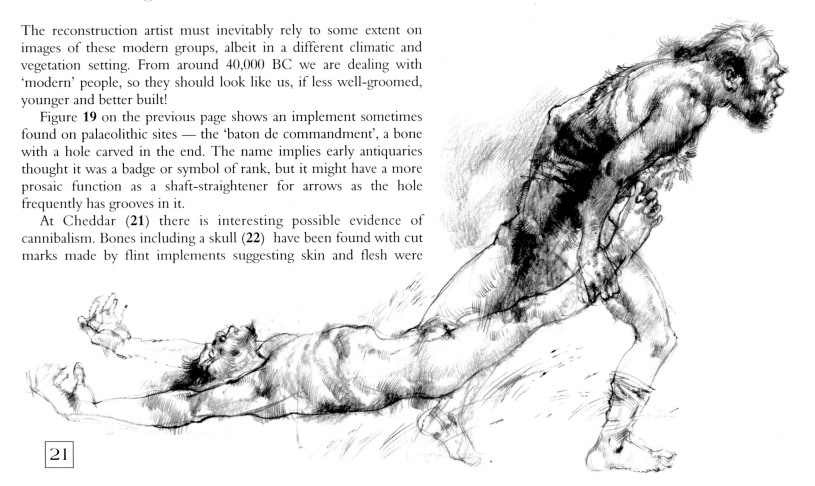

21

removed from the bones. This immediately makes us think of gruesome feasts with one group of early hunting people eating another — or eating their dead relatives! However, the flesh may not have been eaten, and even if it was we cannot assume it was done in an irreverent way. And of course there may be other explanations for the cut marks . . .

Neolithic and Bronze Ages

Following the introduction of agriculture and pasture farming into Britain around 4000 BC, a settled lifestyle with perhaps a more regular food supply became possible. The Neolithic (or New Stone Age) and the succeeding Bronze Age, from around 4000 BC down to 1500 1300 BC is distinguished in the archaeological record by vast numbers of burial, ceremonial and ritual monuments — all associated with monuments to the dead and probable religious centres. There is far more obvious evidence for attention to the dead than of the settlements and fields of the living.

Considerable care was taken with burial, seeming to indicate a concern for the afterlife. Figure **23** shows a reconstruction of a small child buried in a grave at Winterbourne Gunner, in the centre of a circular monument, defined by a ditch, which was probably a round barrow. The child is shown buried on a cloth (or leather), fully clothed with offerings of fruit and flowers.

(Above) Skull from Gough's Cave, Cheddar with cut marks made by flint implements

(Below) Inverted urn with cremated bone from Winterbourne Gunner, Wiltshire

(Above) Probable Bronze Age child burial, Winterbourne Gunner, Wiltshire. (Below) The stages of cremation

26

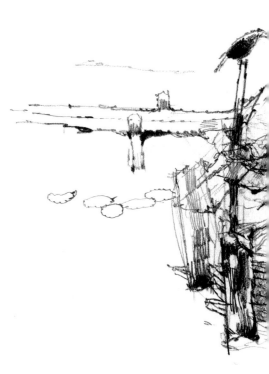

Greylake, Somerset.

26 shows the possible arrangements of a timber walkway at the site while 27 is of a burial platform based on the human bones found

Obviously only the skeleton was found in the excavation but it seems unlikely that some offering was not made at the time before the body was covered in soil. This is the sort of debate and suggestion which the reconstruction artist has to undertake.

From a slightly later date is figure **25**, also from Winterbourne Gunner in Wiltshire. This shows a pyre built to cremate an individual, whose ashes were then put in a large Bronze-Age urn which was then buried upside down (or inverted) in a round hole in the ground (**24**). Evidence for the square-roofed cover was not found in the excavation but some sort of structure over the top is a possibility.

Usually cremated and smashed-up bones (they have to be smashed up to get them in the pot) mean that we can learn very little about the

individual involved. At Winterbourne Gunner many of the key bones were represented and Jacqui MacKinley was able to analyse them and show that this was the burial of a young, rather well-built male.

At Greylake in Somerset (**26** and **27**) a timber structure was excavated in the peat lands adjacent to an area of slightly raised ground. The wood and evidence of contemporary vegetation was preserved in the waterlogged conditions. So well preserved were some of the timbers that a felling date from one oak plank was obtained, by dendrochronology or tree-ring dating, of around 900 BC.

Several human bones were found in the excavation, a rib and an arm bone (**29**), and the farmer had found a skull from roughly the same place in the field prior to the excavation.

It is therefore at least possible that we have here a sort of burial platform used to expose bodies out on the edge of the marsh, reached along a timber trackway. The bodies would have rotted and been picked to pieces by birds and animals. When clean the bones could be

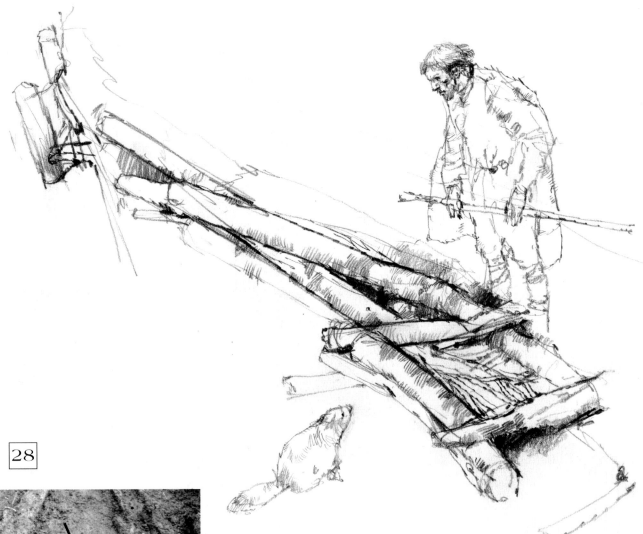

(Below) Greylake —
Human rib and humerus
among the preserved wood

28

collected and buried or disposed of in what was considered to be the appropriate manner. An attempt to show this has been made by the reconstruction artist though the exact details of the structure were unclear and there may of course be other explanations for the bones. We are here relying on analogy with other sites, and indeed ethnographic parallels elsewhere.

Some of the timbers from the Somerset Levels show evidence of beaver teeth marks suggesting that people used timbers from dams and lodges constructed by these animals in local rivers of the Bronze Age. The dilemma of what built the structures is demonstrated above!

3 Later Prehistoric

By the later Prehistoric period we know a great deal more about the lives of the people. They were efficient farmers, good potters and excellent craftsmen. Many of their settlements are known, surrounded by fields and dominated from the late Bronze Age by hillforts with surrounding banks and ditches.

Kemerton, Worcestershire — reconstruction with round houses and enclosing fence

30

31

Iron Age people

From the late Bronze Age we get far more evidence for settlements and fields, and thus the day-to-day lives of people at the time, than we have been able to retrieve from the immediately preceding periods. All over Britain from 1000 BC there are settlements either surviving as field monuments (on Dartmoor for example) or as cropmarks visible on aerial photographs.

Figure **30** shows several round houses, animal pens, a fodder stack (right back), people and various craft activities. This is based on Kemerton in Worcestershire, where excavation of a cropmark site in the Avon valley produced abundant late Bronze Age pottery and even more evidence for succeeding Iron Age activity.

Classical authors tell us about the appearance of the people, with tattoos or body paints (**31**), and we have swords, spears and shields from the period. We also know of textiles and brooches, so more confident attempts can be made at reconstructing clothing. We perhaps forget, looking at the lad at the front, that many warriors were probably quite young.

We know of many round houses from patterns of post-holes found in excavations, and some of the largest and most impressive seem to have been the residences of 'aristocratic' farmers surrounded by *banjo* enclosures (**32**).

A reconstruction of a 'banjo enclosure'in Iron Age Wessex. The term comes from the shape of the enclosing bank and ditch with the parallel banks up to the entrance. Inside is a large roundhouse

A number of such Iron Age houses have been replicated, notably at Butser Ancient Farm in Hampshire. The reconstruction here shows the main house, which probably served a number of functions, surrounded by agricultural and industrial activities (some of which are represented in the archaeological record) but here including totem poles emphasising the status of the family living here. The 'arm' of the banjo would have provided a dramatic entrance along a passageway leading to the gate and main house.

On the previous page (**32**) is a typical Iron Age round house based on excavated evidence and the numerous full scale replicas which have now been built. It is clear that these were substantial houses (not the meagre 'huts' of much literature) with plenty of accommodation for an extended family (*if* they all lived in *one* house). Often there is a porch as shown here, invariably facing south-east. The walls seem to have been of wattle and daub (a mixture of clay, straw or dung). Inside was a fire and an oven but the roof has no chimney. Poorer reconstructions often show a hole at the top of the roof for the smoke to go out; this would have drawn the fire like a chimney, setting fire to the roof. In fact the

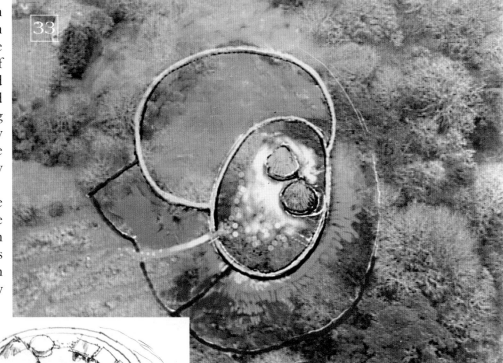

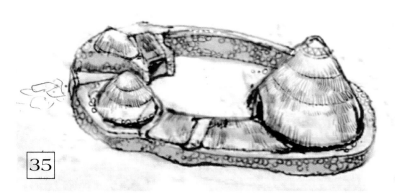

(*Above*)   *Boleigh aerial view reconstruction. Graphics by Victor based on an air photograph*

(*Left*)   *Boleigh, rescan of the central enclosure with round houses and agricultural buildings*

(*Below*)   *Two possible reconstructions of Cornish courtyard houses*

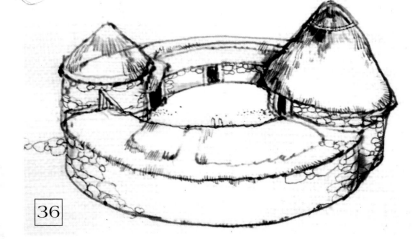

smoke finds its way out through the thatch, keeping it clear of vermin on the way, and smoking any meat or fish hung up in the roof space. Experiments have shown the steeper the pitch the thinner the thatch needed, and the less smoke accumulation. The next few reconstructions show some of the problems faced by archaeologists in interpreting a site and hence the difficulties for the reconstruction artist in painting what the site might have looked like.

The site at Boleigh, near Land's End in Cornwall, was a fogou or underground chamber (really more of a tunnel) and dates from the last few centuries BC and on into the Roman period.

It was clear from excavations that the fogou was connected to a settlement, as they are elsewhere, confined within an enclosure. Figure **33** shows an air view with modern features removed and a settlement drawn in. The fogou was under the centre of this enclosure and probably led out under the enclosure wall.

The settlement might have looked like figure **34**, one of the artist's unfinished working drawings, with an enclosure with an entrance, several round houses and various animal and storage buildings and structures. However, in this part of Cornwall there is a particular type of late Iron Age and Roman period settlement called a 'courtyard house'. These have what seems to have been an open space or yard with one large round room and several other rooms enclosed within a thick encircling wall. Figures **35** and **36** represent the two possible reconstructions of what these houses might have looked like. (One has been 'restored' at Chysauster in West Cornwall.) While this is useful as it gives us some idea of what these buildings might have looked like, other reconstructions are possible, such as the whole complex being covered by one large roof!

In large areas of Britain from around 500 BC a great number of hillforts were built and many, in Wessex and the Welsh Border areas, for example, seem to have continued in use down to the Roman conquest. Hillforts may in fact be something of a

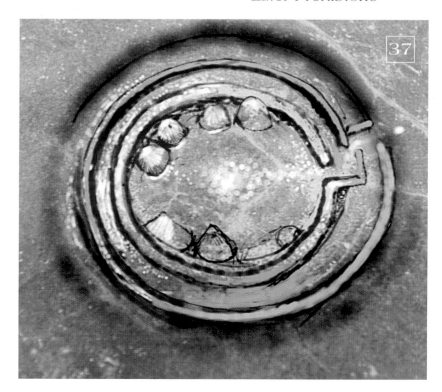

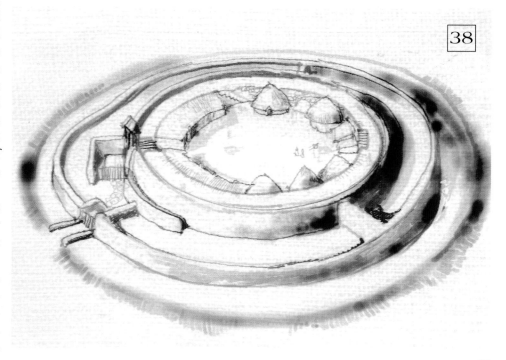

misnomer. While they *now* appear to be essentially defensive, with often massive ramparts, elaborate entrances and complicated ditch systems, there could equally have been an intention to impress and overawe with all these elaborate earthworks. They were designed principally to look impressive.

However, such sites are, more than anything else, settlements, probably where tribal leaders lived, and centres of storage, craft and industrial activities.

Figures **37** and **38** are two views of a circular Cornish hillfort at Chun Castle near Land's End. Here the walls are built of stone, the fort is circular and there is a complex entrance. The interior has buildings and when excavated produced evidence of tin working.

4 The Roman period

The Roman period is a favourite with reconstruction artists. We know so much about the archaeology of the period — indeed there *is* so much archaeology of the Roman period that it is a relatively easy task to depict, even if not to fully understand life at that time. This is because there is a vast amount of material available — from personal adornments through pottery and metal goods to physical building materials, roads, industrial activities and military establishments.

We know a great deal about the Roman army, particularly of the first and second centuries AD. The equipment of legionaries and auxiliary troops has been excavated so that we can get a vivid picture of the soldiers in their regalia.

Overleaf (**41**) is a legionary standard bearer, while figure **40** shows a cavalry officer. These troops occupied numerous fortresses, forts and fortlets, many of which have been excavated.

The conquest by Roman troops in AD 43 and the taking over of south-east Britain by the armies up to AD 47 is reasonably well understood. In figure **39** a detachment of the army is about to cross the Thames. These troops are legionaries, with shield and spear, while the main character (right) is a centurion. At the back, surprisingly, elephants are shown, though it does appear they were brought in as part of the psychological warfare and used as 'tanks' and lookouts.

39

The Roman army crossing the Thames in the conquest period

40

41

(Above) Roman Light Cavalry, from my book on 'Horses in Battle'. Stirrups were not known to the Romans, and this limited their effectiveness in fighting on horseback against the Huns — V

The standard bearer of the Legion, the carrier of the 'Eagle'. They wore animal skins over their heads, which gave them an even more sinister appearence. Leopard skins were worn originally, but may have been replaced by wolf or bear skin in Britain — V

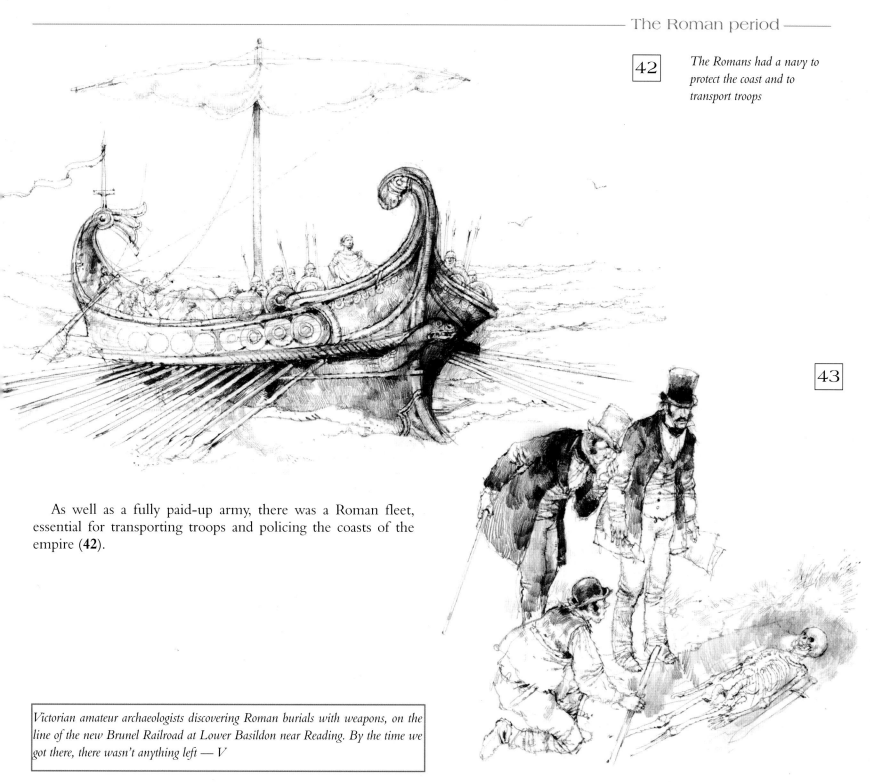

The Romans had a navy to protect the coast and to transport troops

43

As well as a fully paid-up army, there was a Roman fleet, essential for transporting troops and policing the coasts of the empire (**42**).

Victorian amateur archaeologists discovering Roman burials with weapons, on the line of the new Brunel Railroad at Lower Basildon near Reading. By the time we got there, there wasn't anything left — V

Basildon Roman villa

How do we know so much about the Roman period? Partly because the archaeology is so obvious with masses of finds, especially pottery, building debris and coins, on any Roman site. Also education in the eighteenth and nineteenth centuries, especially of the aristocracy, gentry and upper classes, was based on the Classics — Latin and Greek — and so an interest in aspects of the classical tradition was fostered from the eighteenth century at least. In the railway building boom of the mid-nineteenth century many previously unknown archaeological sites were disturbed but it was usually only the Roman sites that were recognized for what they were. On the previous page railway engineers and workmen look at remains unearthed near Basildon, Berkshire, when Brunel was building the main Great Western line in 1838. We now know that this was part of a villa complex in the Thames valley in the pleasant landscape of the Goring Gap (**43**).

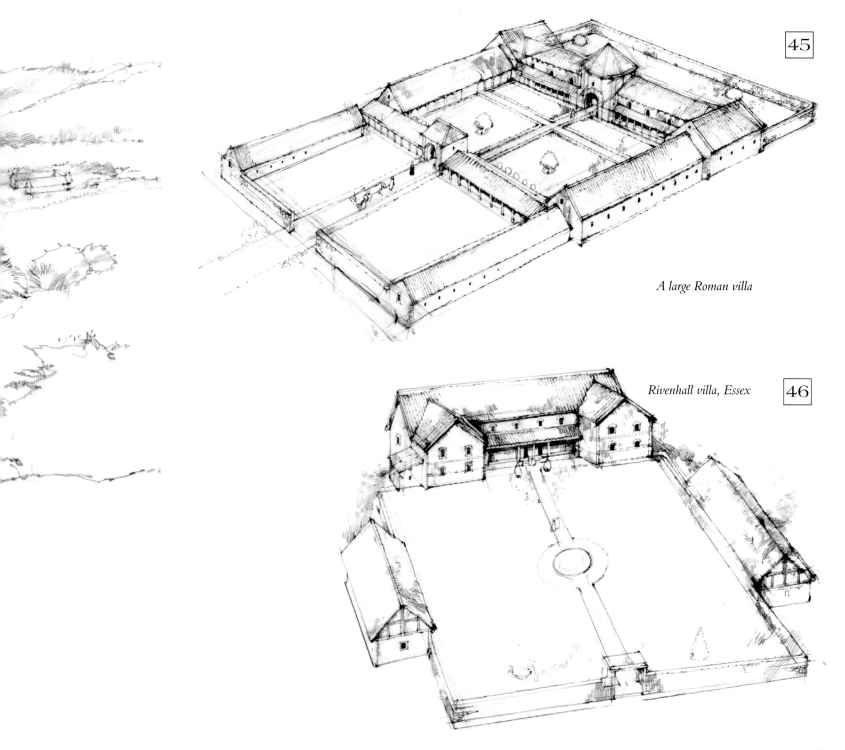

45

A large Roman villa

Rivenhall villa, Essex 46

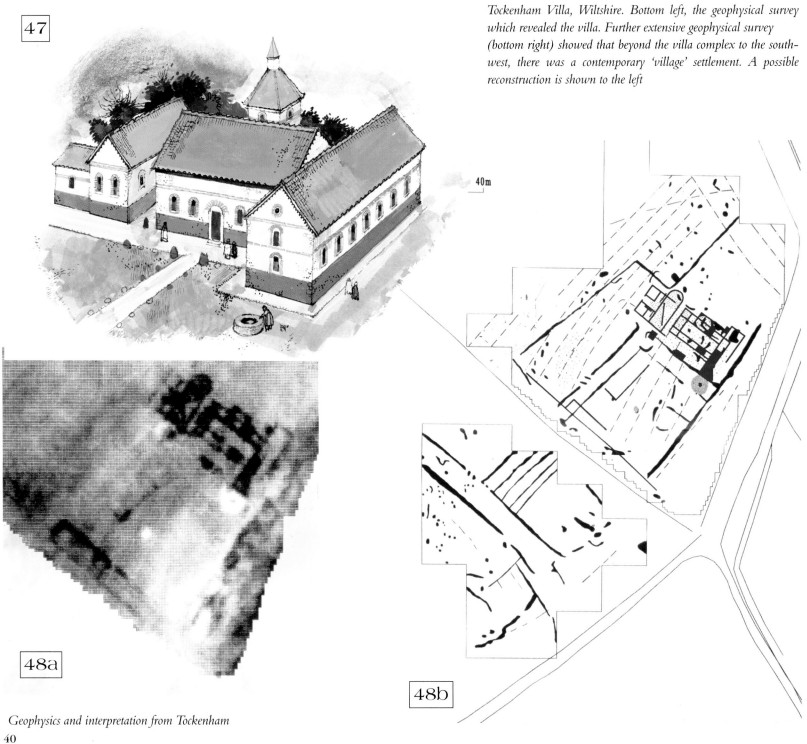

47

Tockenham Villa, Wiltshire. Bottom left, the geophysical survey which revealed the villa. Further extensive geophysical survey (bottom right) showed that beyond the villa complex to the south-west, there was a contemporary 'village' settlement. A possible reconstruction is shown to the left

40m

48a

48b

Geophysics and interpretation from Tockenham

The reconstruction (44) suggests a mainly wooded landscape with pasture rather than arable fields. Environmental evidence elsewhere in the Thames valley tells us that these meadowlands beside the river were largely used for pastoral farming at this time so it is reasonable to suggest that the land was a series of grass fields. Little detail can be shown of the buildings as subsequent railway development seems to have obliterated the central complex of the villa.

Villas came in a variety of sizes and plans, reflecting their different origins and roles as everything from farms and bailiff's houses up to substantial and opulent rural palaces lived in by provincial governors, client kings and Roman administrators.

Figure 45 provides an artistic reconstruction of a very large complex with several ranges of one- or two-storey buildings providing the main accommodation. In front (to the left) are extensive formal gardens of paths, lawns, standard bushes and low box hedges, evidence for all of which has been recovered from excavations. The main path leads to the fine entrance hall of the villa where guests and officials would have been greeted.

Beyond the garden, under an impressive gatehouse, a further yard accommodated stables for horses, storage buildings for agricultural produce and workshops.

The second example (46) is based on a villa at Rivenhall in Essex.

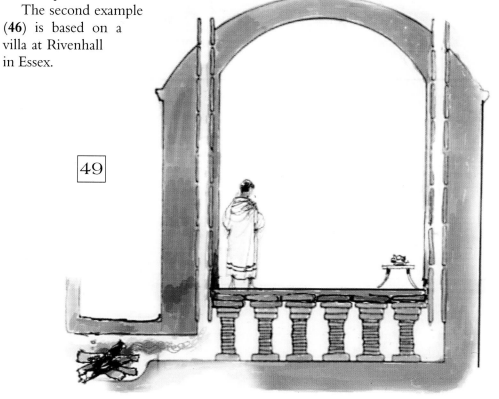

(Above) A highly-coloured household god in a niche in the wall

(Left) A hypocaust heating system. The fire provides warm air for underfloor and wall heating

51

Here a more modest house with a verandah and a couple of projecting wings faces another garden which has other, probable storage and accommodation buildings on each side. Much of this villa was excavated by Warwick and Kirsty Rodwell and so we can be sure of a lot of the detail.

With so many excavations of villas in the past, it is possible for reconstruction artists to have a good attempt at reconstructing sites for which we have little information or where only small-scale excavations have been carried out. Evidence of roofing and walling materials, stucco and plaster work, floors, heating systems and statuary often survive so that the details of a reconstruction will be there even if the overall arrangement of buildings on the site is less certain; it is not always clear, for example, how the complex of buildings, yards and gardens developed over time, during the several hundred years when some sites were in existence. Just like today we would expect extensions, alterations and demolitions.

This can be seen in a site excavated at Tockenham in Wiltshire. The reconstruction **47** is based on very little excavation evidence, much of the site had been damaged by ploughing, but the geophysical survey for the site was exceptionally clear (see **48a** and **b**) showing

(Above) Making offerings to the household god in the house

the *general* outline and shape of the buildings, though not their chronology. Details of painted plaster walls and roofing materials are reasonably certain, as is the existence of a hypocaust heating system (**49**). In this, ceramic tile pillars were used to support stone or concrete floors so that hot air from fires in stokeholes alongside could warm the room. Hot gases passed through flue tiles in the wall and out through vents or chimneys.

At least one room must have been used as a shrine with a household god represented by a carved panel. This now survives built into the south wall of the medieval church where it has been wrongly identified as Aesculapius. Dr Martin Henig is sure it was painted brightly (**50**) and resided in a niche in the wall. Offerings would have been made before it to ensure the good fortune of the resident family (**51**).

52

As in so many cases, this piece of Roman sculpture surviving in the church is not the only piece that has survived from Roman times. As work progressed on the villa at Tockenham, the farmer remarked that he had a stone 'fish head' which had been assumed to be eighteenth-century. This has now been confidently identified as Roman as well, almost certainly from the villa and probably a water spout or fountainhead bringing water into a basin or garden pond (**52**). The reconstruction shown here is one of a number of possibilities of how this head could have been mounted and used.

53

A Roman kitchen based on a site at Preston St Mary

Women with a polished, silvered bronze mirror

54

From the finds of everyday items, details of personal life can often be reconstructed; here (**54**) a servant girl or daughter is holding up a mirror to her mother or mistress. A piece of such a highly-polished bronze mirror was found in excavations at Papcastle in Cumbria. We are used to seeing ourselves in mirrors and in photographs (and increasingly on videos or even television) but it was much more difficult in the past; highly-polished reflecting surfaces, and of course water reflection, were the best that could be done.

The vast quantities of Roman pottery and other domestic equipment found on many Roman sites, together with food remains (or at least, bones) and the existence of Roman cookery texts, means that we have a good idea about Roman diet, cookery and food preparation. Illustrated above is a Roman kitchen based on a site at Preston St Mary, Suffolk, with pots on a stove fired with charcoal on a raised platform, large storage pots, which would have held beans and peas and grain, onions or garlic hanging up and other jars for liquids, herbs and such like.

As well as villas, which we should probably think of as the farms and country houses of the Roman rural landscape, many towns were developed. Some of these grew up serving forts but stayed to provide local services when the army moved on. Others were Romanized developments of 'Celtic' tribal centres, yet others were built-up industrial and agricultural centres.

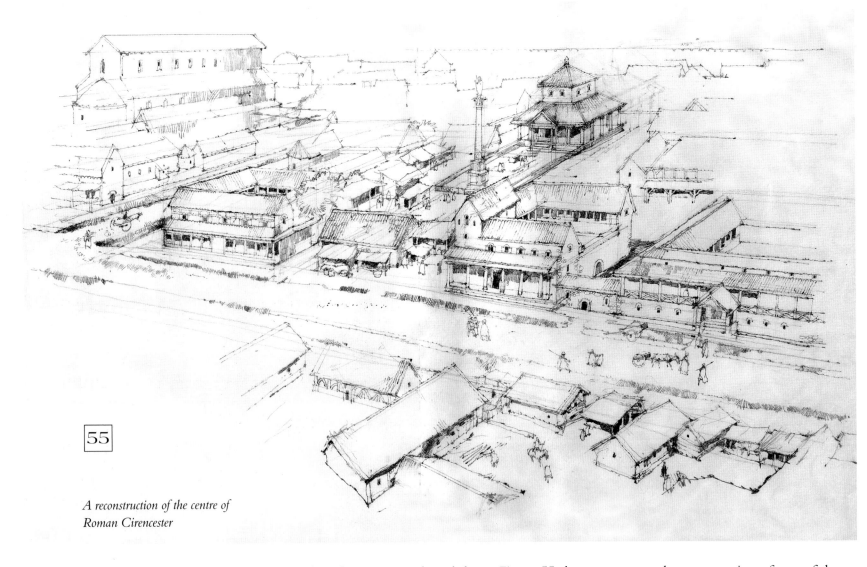

55

*A reconstruction of the centre of
Roman Cirencester*

They acquired shops, offices, town halls, market places, inns and workshops. Figure **55** shows a suggested reconstruction of part of the centre of Cirencester based on considerable excavated evidence over the last three to four decades. It shows rows of shops, some colonnaded with houses and properties behind. To the left is the town hall with the marketplace alongside; in the centre is a temple with a 'Jupiter column' in front — a monument to the Roman emperors. Beyond is a hint of the town wall, which any town of any consequence would have had.

One of the main functions of these towns in a commercial economy using money as a means of exchange was to provide markets where goods could be bought and sold. There was much greater division of labour in the Roman period with people specializing in all sorts of crafts, industrial activity and the production of certain goods and services.

Two examples of this are shown here. In the Weald of south-east England, a flourishing and large-scale iron production industry was developed based on abundant iron ore and a plentiful supply of wood for charcoal fuel. Below right, large numbers of furnaces are in operation smelting the iron ore to produce a lump (or bloom) of iron which could then be hammered into shape.

In the middle of this site at Beauport Park in Sussex, a bathhouse was constructed (**58**) and this seems to have been the only solidly built building on the site, presumably for the use of officials who organized the industry who seem to have been from the *Classis Britannica*, the Roman fleet, if the tiles stamped on the site are to be believed.

The bathhouse of Beauport Park, Sussex

Iron smelting in the Weald in clay furnaces

59

We presumably therefore have a site which would have been run by high-ranking officials and officers in the navy (**59**) but where the work was done by 'armies' of labourers who probably did not have access to the bath suite.

The little reconstruction drawing (**60**) shows two recognizable bathers (Mick Aston and Tony Robinson) waiting to go into the sequence of rooms in the bathhouse!

As well as increased industrial production there were numerous improvements in farming technique. To the right is shown one possibility — the *tribulum* — a board 'armed' with cutting flint blades used for threshing crops to extract the grain from the stalks. These can still be seen in use in various parts of Europe today. Figure **62** shows blades being made from flint nodules by a flint knapper and then hammered into wooden boards which have grooves cut in them. Figure **61** is the *tribulum* with a stone block (to weigh it down) being pulled over a crop by a horse.

During the Roman period, Christianity was introduced and then adopted as the official state religion. Before that however there was a pantheon of gods and a variety of temples and complexes in which they were worshipped. Figures **63** and **64** show aspects of this. Each temple, usually a square building with a walkway around it, and housing the statues and symbols of the god or gods worshipped here, lay in a courtyard surrounded by a walled enclosure (the *temenos*). Within this would have been one or more (outdoor) altars, stalls selling offerings and trinkets (rather like gift shops in cathedrals today) together with buildings for priests and places where visitors (who were in effect pilgrims) could stay.

Figure **63** is a reconstruction of a very important temple found in Greenwich Park. This may have been an Imperial temple; certainly an inscription found here suggests worship of former emperors. Priests would have conducted the sacrifices and offerings. Figure **64** depicts a similar temple at Canterbury within the Roman city with the sacrifice of a chicken and goat about to take place at the outdoor altar officiated over by the gowned and hooded priest.

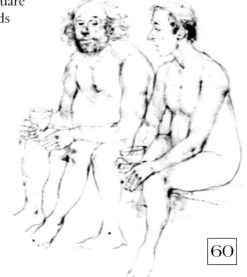

60

Using the tribulum. *Experiments showed the stone was not needed*

61

A drawing of Peter Reynolds and Phil Harding working on the tribulum. *I have 'Romanised' their costume — V*

Making a tribulum

62

63

Reconstruction of the temple, altars and
temenos *(enclosure) of the site in*
Greenwich Park

Canterbury — a sacrifice taking place at an altar in the temple precinct

65

(Above) Roman funeral procession.

(Right) Burial of a child in Roman York

While burial for much of the Roman period was in the form of cremations, ashes being buried in pots or glass vessels, inhumation burial (in graves) comes in, in the later part of the Roman period, perhaps associated with the introduction of Christianity. In figure **65** we can see such a funeral procession bringing a body to be buried in a cemetery. These were always outside the settled areas and may be associated with temples or mausolea. Figure **66** is the burial of a child in a coffin at a circular mausoleum at York. Offerings are being prepared and offered at the graveside. Such a scene should remind us of the large percentage of infants and children who died early on in all periods, up to the twentieth century.

Here we found a burial of a small child among others, with evidence of a huge mausoleum behind it. The picture was done in a day under some pressure — V

66

5 A Dark Age?

The period after the Roman interlude is a difficult one to work on. It used to be called the Dark Ages — it is still very difficult to see much of the archaeology of the times, whether it be finds or buildings and structures. For much of the period 400-1100 many areas have no pottery for archaeologists to interpret and other tangible traces are equally difficult to find.

This period is different in each part of the country. The south-east and eastern areas were overrun with pagan Saxon culture; the Roman Christian lifestyle and economy (which may only ever have been skin deep) where it had lasted was replaced by pagan burial practices, habitations of wood (halls and sunken-floored buildings) and the use of more organic (i.e. rottable!) materials for everyday objects. So the archaeology we find is usually in graves and settlements discovered by accident.

The following few figures give an example of this from Winterbourne Gunner in Wiltshire. Foundations dug for a new house unearthed a number of pagan Saxon burials. One was of a woman who probably held a high status in the local community. Figure **67** shows the burial of the woman in the grave and also the sort of ceremony which may have taken place at the graveside with offerings of flowers and fruit (**68**).

There were a few hints from finds of pagan Saxon pottery that there was a contemporary settlement not far away. Figures **69** and **70** show the cemetery beyond the settlement and a suggestion of the timber houses which we find elsewhere from this period. Despite regular burials, life goes on (**70**).

In the north and west, in areas which were never perhaps fully Romanized and parts of the civil provinces, the picture is rather different with local chieftains reoccupying hill forts; Christianity seems to have continued. There is even less pottery, finds or structural evidence to be located in these areas.

The art of the period, on burial objects and jewellery, and in the west on stone monuments and crosses as

Winterbourne Gunner burial of a woman

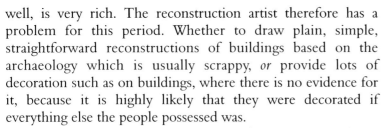

The Winterbourne Gunner burial cemetery (above) and the contemporary settlement (below

well, is very rich. The reconstruction artist therefore has a problem for this period. Whether to draw plain, simple, straightforward reconstructions of buildings based on the archaeology which is usually scrappy, *or* provide lots of decoration such as on buildings, where there is no evidence for it, because it is highly likely that they were decorated if everything else the people possessed was.

Figure **73** represents an attempt to work with these problems. Many small defensive sites were reoccupied in the west and north after the Roman period and became the bases of local chieftains (called *tyrants* by the chroniclers). The basic building seems to have been a large barn-like hall, which provided the living accommodation. This reconstruction shows some decoration of the timber-work of the hall. It also shows a timber palisade reinforcing the earthwork defences, and timber gate towers. When there is so little evidence available, a drawing like this really represents a model of our current thoughts rather than an accurate reconstruction of any particular site.

Rather more is known of the example shown in figures **71** and **72**. At Llangorse in South Wales is the only crannog so far known in England and Wales, though there are lots in Scotland and Ireland. A crannog is an artificial island built from dumped clay and stones on which is built a house and farm buildings. Often they are of very high status, belonging to kings and princes, and this one seems to have been the headquarters of the kings of Brycheiniog (now Brecon). Some excavations, by Dr Mark Redknap for the National Museum of Wales, have taken place on the site. The views show the plank walkway to the island, a gateway, palisades (of which many timbers still remain preserved in the waterlogged conditions of the lake) and several large rectangular hall-like buildings. Just because all this was built of timber rather than stone does not mean it would not have looked magnificent and impressive.

In the east of the country, Anglo-Saxon paganism continued with bodies buried with grave goods, such as swords, knives, beads, brooches and probably food — all of which it was thought would be useful in the next world and would show the status of the deceased.

Some burials were immensely rich, figure **75** for example, at Sutton Hoo, in Suffolk in East Anglia, where a great burial ship was excavated in 1939. Although all signs of the body had totally disappeared because of the local soil conditions, vast numbers of objects survived and now grace a magnificent display in the British Museum. The reconstruction here shows people manoeuvring the ship into position over the burial with the grave goods, with onlookers (or mourners) and the surrounding cemetery of burial mounds. The individual burial may well have been a local king — Raedwald of the Wuffingas who died in the seventh century has been suggested. The long Anglo-Saxon poem *Beowulf* gives the flavour of the occasion of such a burial, though in this case a cremation under a barrow.

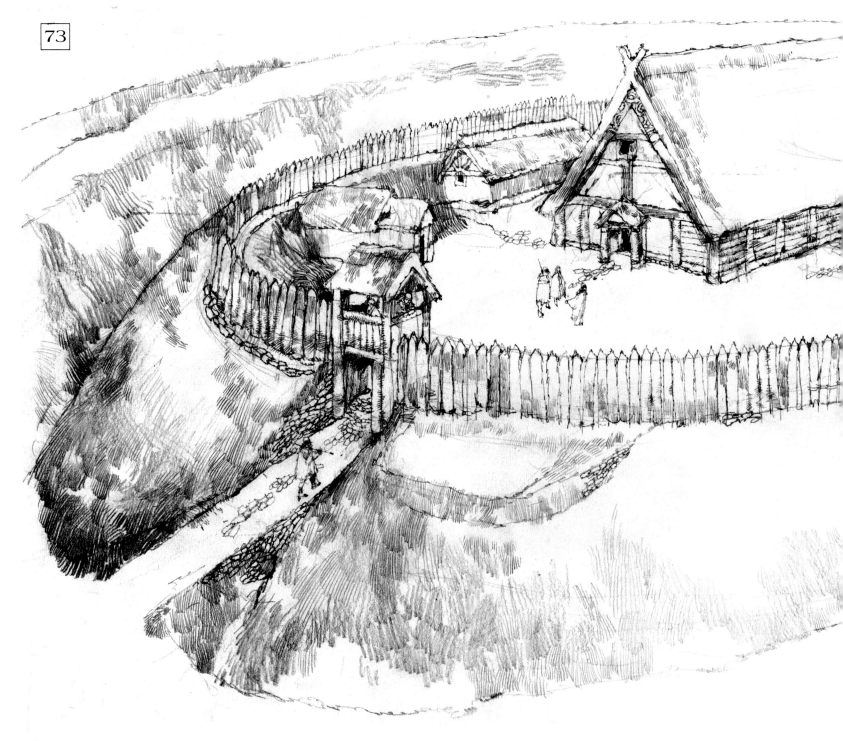

73

Then on the headland, the Geats prepared a mighty pyre
For Beowulf, hung round with helmets and shields
and shining mail, in accordance with his wishes;
and then the mourning warriors laid
their dear lord, the famous prince, upon it.

Then the Geats built a barrow on the headland —
It was high and broad, visible from far
To all seafarers; in ten days they built the beacon
For that courageous man; and they constructed
As noble an enclosure as wise men
Could devise; to enshrine the ashes.
They buried rings and brooches in the barrow,

All those adornments that brave men
Had brought out from the hoard after Beowulf died.
They bequeathed the gleaming gold, treasures of men,
To the earth, and there it still remains
As useless to men as it was before.

Quoted from *Beowulf: A verse translation* by Kevin Crossley-Holland (Oxford, 1999, pages 104 & 105).

er hall and gatehouse with surrounding palisade. A 'model' of the sort of reoccupied site we find in western Britain

Christianity was reintroduced into England in the sixth and seventh centuries and spread by missionaries converting local kings and their subjects. Many individual kings and members of their royal families were thought of as saints, particularly if they were murdered, and came to be regarded as martyrs. The progress of conversion was very much a series of miracles.

One of the ship burials at the Sutton Hoo site. A large number of different burials took place. This is one with the body placed under the boat — V

Drawn on a lovely, sunny day on the very same road where it was said to have happened. The drawing took an afternoon — V

Figure **74** shows part of the legend of St Aethelbert who was murdered in 794. He wanted to marry Aelfryth, daughter of King Offa of Mercia. Offa's wife, Coenfryth, persuaded Offa to have Aethelbert (who was the Christian king of East Anglia) murdered in case any of the offspring of the marriage usurped the portion of any of Offa's sons. Aethelbert's head was cut off and as the body was taken away on a cart, the head rolled off. It was retrieved by a blind man who regained his sight (the miracle) and then chased after the cart — the scene shown — in order to replace the head. The remains were buried at Hereford which became a cult centre for St Aethelbert. Such incidents are numerous in the Anglo-Saxon records and such scenes may have been common!

While there were cathedrals and churches, much of the Christian mission was carried out from monasteries. We know relatively little about these as there is so little archaeological evidence available for most of them. Rather more evidence for monasteries at this period survives in Ireland and the following figures show an example at Downpatrick, County Down. The reconstructions are based on the local topography (almost an island in a formerly flooded area (**76**)), a good geophysical survey and a series of carefully targeted excavations. Because there was a later medieval monastery and cathedral on the site (**78**), the main early monastery reconstruction is inevitably based on other contemporary monasteries (**77**) of which we know more.

Figure **77** shows a series of concentric circular enclosures, the inner one containing the church (or several churches), a round tower and a number of high crosses and burials. Around this are shown the 'cells' or small houses of the monks, other communal buildings and industrial activities. Much of this activity continued (**78**) when the main buildings were rebuilt in the more conventional monastic plan. Here we can see a larger church, a cloister and other conventual buildings. Beyond is a gatehouse, which pilgrims would have approached after a ferry journey, and other industrial buildings, parts of which were excavated.

We know that monasteries were centres of learning and scholarship. Christianity is based on a book — the Bible — it is a literate religion. But printing was not yet invented so the only way for the monks (or nuns) to make copies of the Bible and other texts involved the laborious preparation of skins for vellum, and the copying out, writing and illuminating of texts. Scenes such as **79** must have been common in all the larger and better-equipped monasteries of the British Isles. Some very fine books survive of course, such as the *Lindisfarne Gospels* and the *Book of Kells*, but archaeology usually only recovers the metal bits from the cover (book clasps), pens (*styli*) and traces of the pigments and palettes used.

We tend to forget that any monastery (or royal palace) could only exist so long as a food supply was procured to feed the inmates, monks or nuns (or royal family). The people who did the work — agricultural or industrial — tend to be forgotten by history and yet they made up the bulk of the population and did the lion's share of the work. Figure **80** (overleaf) encapsulates this idea — the swineherd feeding and looking after the (rather primitive looking) pigs — a staple food, killed and salted down or smoked for use over the winter.

79   *A monastic scribe at work at his desk*

80

Early monks had to do the dirty work as well. I went to the Venerable Bede's Museum and Farm Centre at Jarrow where they had some of the original breeds, including the lovely but quite ferocious semi-wild boars. I would not envy his job — V

The following group of reconstructions shows both the problems of archaeology and also how much can be learned with skilful examination and analysis. In 1998, at Bawsey in Norfolk, excavations unearthed a skeleton from the Saxon period at a probable monastic site. The top of the head appeared to have been cut off but was buried with the body. It looked like a battle victim — the result of a skirmish between various Saxon groups or the result of a Viking raid. On this basis a reconstruction was produced to illustrate the incident (**81**).

Subsequent study by Professor Margaret Cox of Bournemouth University, however, has generated a totally different view of this incident. Firstly, the person involved was a women and possibly a nun, if the site was a monastery. Certainly she was attacked, from behind, and a deep cut made in her skull (**82**). However, the blow did not kill her — rather she must have lain undetected somewhere for a brief period (overnight?). Analysis of marks on the leg bones of the skeleton showed that at some stage they had been chewed by an animal (**84**). It is possible that this might have happened after death but the body would have been buried making it inaccessible to animals. It is easier to envisage, if difficult to comprehend, that the unconscious body lay (in undergrowth?) long enough to be gnawed. The teeth marks show that it was a badger.

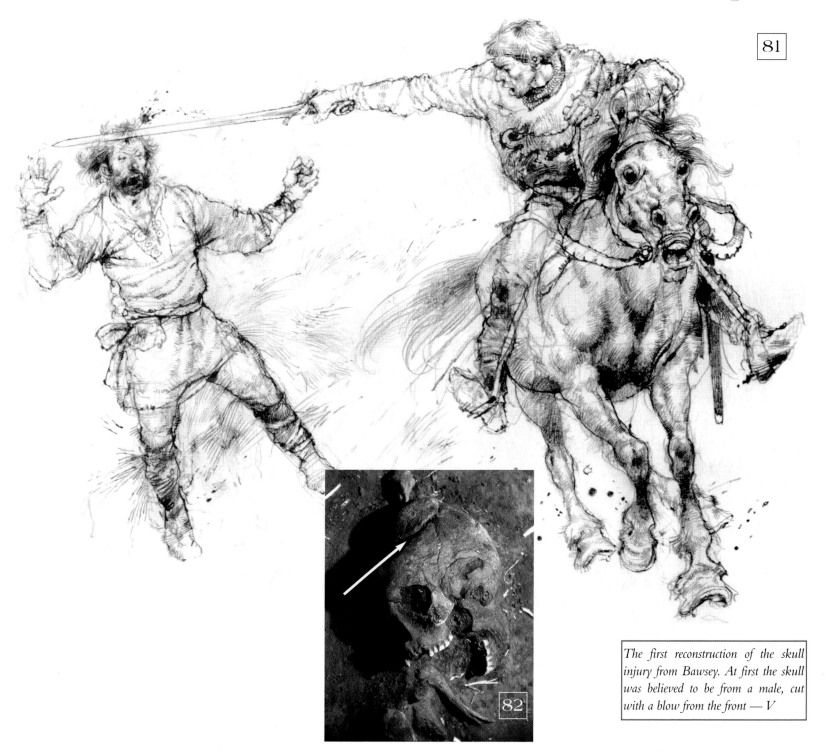

81

82

The first reconstruction of the skull injury from Bawsey. At first the skull was believed to be from a male, cut with a blow from the front — V

Bawsey attack version 2 — the woman is attacked

83

More research identified that the victim was a quite robust lady — very likely a nun. More reconstructions were needed based on the new evidence including badger teeth marks — V

The body is gnawed by a badger (below)

84

The real surprise came from close examination of the separate skull piece. Certainly a metal blade was involved — there is a cut at the back — but it was detached in a medical operation — trepanning or trephination — an ancient technique employed to relieve pressure on the brain and psychological disorders by cutting a round piece out of the skull. Miraculously people often survived and recovered.

Clearly the body had been found, presumably in a terrible state, and then her friends or community had embarked on a brave but ultimately unsuccessful attempt to save her life by carrying out an operation on her skull (**85**). Not surprisingly, given the standards of hygiene at the time, she died before any new bone could develop (as revealed by an examination of the bone edges using a scanning electron microscope) and she was buried still with the detached 'skull cap' to be found 1300 years later.

An example such as this spectacularly shows how much can be learned from bones dug up in an archaeological excavation. Skilled ex--cavation using modern technology, and careful analysis of marks made by teeth, blades and operating tools has revealed a unique incident of great poignancy from the past. Such analysis gets us very close to incidents in the lives of people of that time.

85

Bawsey: the skull operation

86 *The Viking burial at Ness of Brough on Sanday, Orkney*

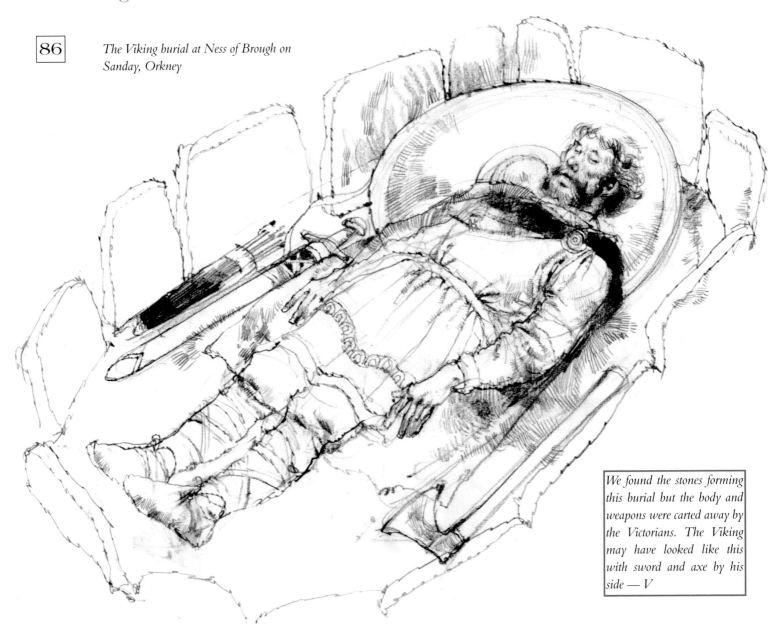

We found the stones forming this burial but the body and weapons were carted away by the Victorians. The Viking may have looked like this with sword and axe by his side — V

From the early 800's life in Britain was increasingly disrupted by ruthless Scandinavian pirates — the Vikings. Relatively, we know a lot more about these people, from both contemporary accounts of them and from the rich finds from their burial sites and settlements. The latter developed when some of them colonized other lands and settled down producing town sites such as York and Dublin in the ninth and tenth centuries.

They came by boat, superb ocean-going vessels which could also navigate the big rivers of Europe. When they died they were often buried in ships or in ship-like graves lined with stones. A reconstruction of one of these, dug into an earlier prehistoric burial mound at

At York we found a lot of items of everyday Viking life, such as beads, pottery and a Viking shoe. These gave me the inspiration for a busy Viking street— V

Viking York with streets and a new church built behind

Ness of Brough on Sanday, Orkney, is shown in **86**. Viking warriors were often buried with their sword, shield, knife and spear supplied for the next world. This grave was partially excavated in the early twentieth century and only relocated in 1997.

Excavations in towns and cities such as York and Dublin, as well as sites in Scandinavia, have shown extensive Viking occupation in these places which were trading and craft centres. York in particular has produced striking evidence of streets lined with rectangular

88

A lot of Viking buildings survived at ground level in York, now part of an excellent museum. The Viking street layout is also there to this day. I reconstructed the houses and an early wooden church — V

89

Keith Prosser made a magnificent bone comb in a very short time. He also made numerous replica Viking artefacts, and looked every inch of a Viking — V

buildings, gable-end on to the street (**87** and **88**). The archaeology shows these were lived in by metal workers, comb-makers, bone-workers, fishermen, woodworkers and so on. Eventually the Vikings adopted Christianity and in figure **87** a new church is shown behind the houses and workshops.

While figure **89** is not strictly speaking a reconstruction drawing since it is based on a modern craftsman wearing replica clothes, it should give an impression of the range of raw materials and tools in use at this time, in this case bone, antler, and ivory from walrus tusks.

6 Medieval

Norman Conquest

In 1066, the Norman Conquest brought Saxon England to an end at the Battle of Hastings (**91**). The result was not a foregone conclusion — after all, Harold had defeated the Vikings just before at Stamford Bridge in Yorkshire — and it was to be some time before William the Conqueror and his successors had a reasonably secure hold on the country.

Many changes followed on from the Norman Conquest. There was a great change of landholders as Saxon thegns were replaced by Norman vassals. Castles seem to have been introduced and most cathedrals, monasteries and churches were rebuilt, replanned and enlarged in the Romanesque style, which we call Norman.

The new social order of society from then on, in the Middle Ages, was seen at the time as divided into three — those who fought, those who prayed and those who worked. We can see these aspects reflected in the next group of reconstruction drawings.

Rather like the Roman period, this is a time for which a lot of reconstruction drawings have been produced. Many castles, cathedrals, monasteries and churches survive from the Middle Ages, and abundant documentation, including elaborately illuminated manuscripts have been preserved in various archives. We therefore know a great deal about what people looked like, what they wore, what tools, equipment and weapons they used, what many of their buildings were like and how they were furnished and decorated.

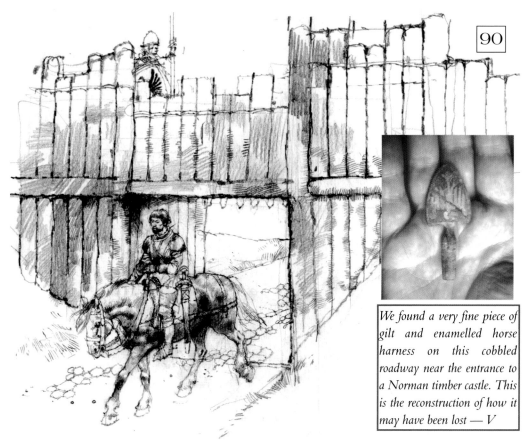

90

We found a very fine piece of gilt and enamelled horse harness on this cobbled roadway near the entrance to a Norman timber castle. This is the reconstruction of how it may have been lost — V

91

Hastings — from the book Horses in Battle. *The Norman cavalry on their huge stallions bore down on the Saxons and decided the outcome of the battle — V*

A working drawing of a medieval peasant's house shared with animals — V

But this is mainly for the middle and upper classes; we know a lot less about the peasant families at the bottom of the social pile. Over the last 50 years though, research on medieval villages, moated sites, peasant houses and farming systems has taught us a great deal about this group as well.

Figure **95** shows a typical medieval village based on a site at High Worsall in North Yorkshire. At the end of the street, which is little more that a muddy well-used alley, is a stone built manor house with a small stone church (to the left). Along each side of the street are series of medieval longhouses with crofts, paddocks, gardens, and orchards behind. Figure **92** is a reconstruction of what the inside of one of these houses might have looked like. The people shared the space with their animals, though they would have been housed beyond a screen (not shown here) downhill from the family. In the middle of the only living room would have been the hearth with a fire for warmth and cooking. The family would have lived and slept around this, though a loft could also have been used for sleeping as well as storage.

Another of these can be seen in **94** which shows a longhouse and its croft at Waddon in Dorset. Much of this was excavated and it remains as an earthwork still.

We can imagine such houses as rather dank, dirty and draughty, with little in the way of furniture or possessions. Excavations however show that they were kept clean and secure and thousands of peasants spent many generations living like this.

Many thousands of such settlements existed and most lie under our 'modern' villages. Several thousand however were deserted in the Middle Ages and later, leaving fields full of earthworks as clues to their former existence. It is the plan of these earthworks that has been used here as the basis for the reconstruction (**95**).

(left) An aerial view of High Worsall showing the enclosure (top) for the church, and the earthworks of the farm sites, with one (foreground) under excavation

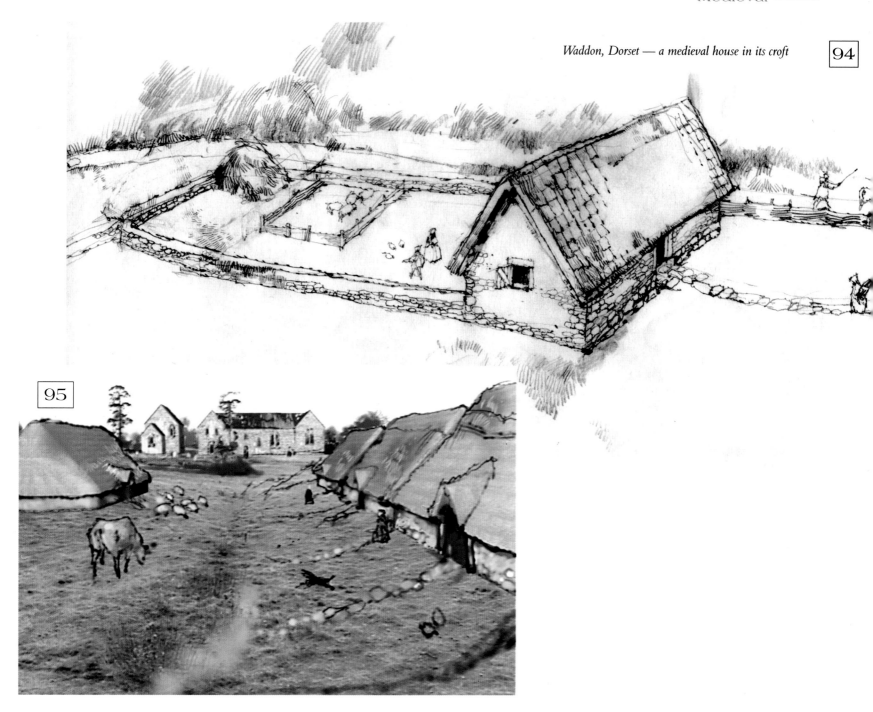

Waddon, Dorset — a medieval house in its croft 94

95

Reconstruction of High Worsall village. At the end of a wide street of houses there is a church (left) and manor house

96

Building the ramparts for a castle

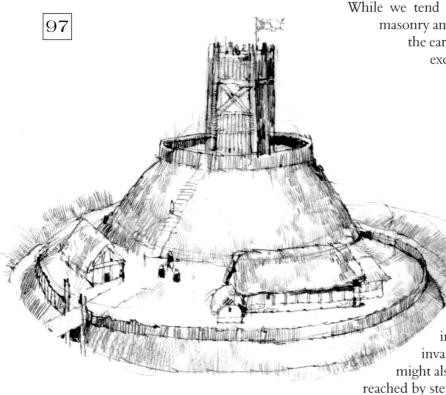

97

While we tend to think of castles as stone structures with elaborate masonry and carefully built keeps, towers and gate-houses, many of the earliest castles were built of earth, with ramparts of material excavated from ditches and topped with timber palisades of split logs or planks for walls. This was hard work involving much earth moving and dumping (**96**), probably carried out by forced Saxon labour, though skilled 'architects' must have been involved in the layout and direction of the work.

Motte and bailey castles were the normal type of castle (**97** left) though *ring works* were common and seem to owe something to late Saxon traditions. Both involved an enclosure defended by a ditch, banks and palisade, and each contained halls, service buildings, stores and so on, to sustain the family or garrison living there, and there would generally be a chapel and perhaps a gatehouse to control entry as well.

Mottes, the great earthen mounds, were either an intrinsic part of the design or added later. They were invariably surmounted by a timber lookout tower which might also include some accommodation. This would have been reached by steps or a bridge from the bailey (or inner rampart). While some mottes are only a matter of a few metres high, the biggest (such as those at Thetford, Ewyas Harold or Richards Castle) are colossal and must have involved a lot of heavy labour. Inside (**98** right) halls would have been built of stone in some cases, or more often timber framing on stone foundations.

Figure **99** shows a reconstruction drawing of Alderton in Northamptonshire. This is a ringwork castle that does not appear to have had any stone structure associated with it (later on a stone gatehouse was built). The massive ramparts and deep ditches enclose a roughly oval area which would have been defended by timber palisades, one or more towers (one is shown here at the highest point) and a timber gatehouse defending the only entrance. Sometimes, as here, there were subsidiary enclosures for corralling animals, and providing temporary accommodation. Inside can be seen a large hall (built in a rather antiquated style), kitchen, private accommodation — the hall itself was a very *public*

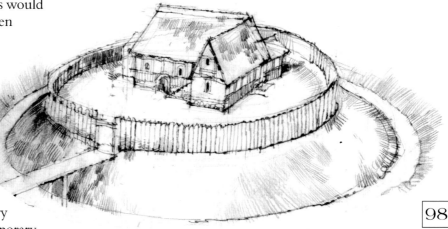

98

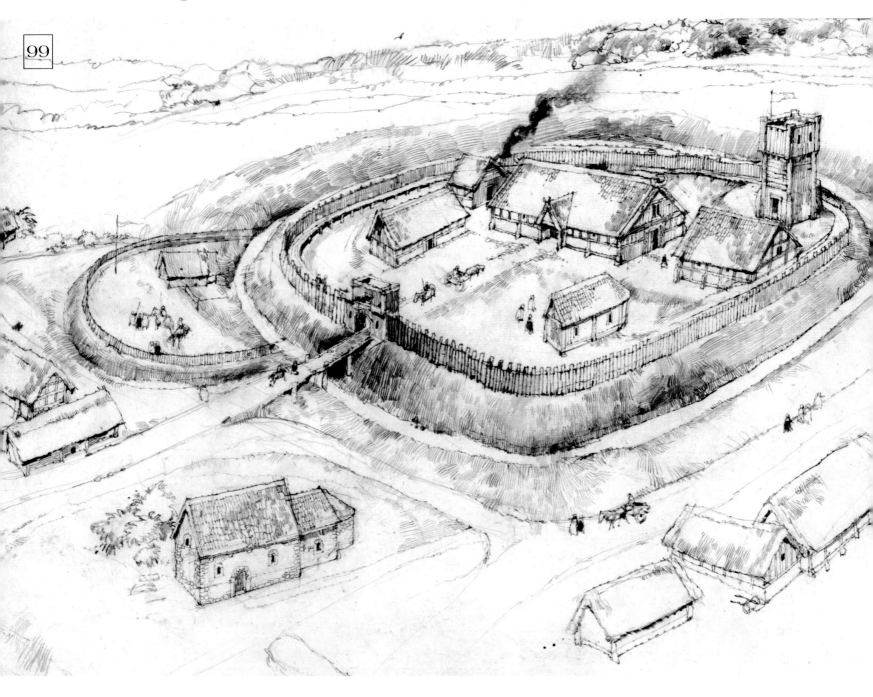

Alderton, Northamptonshire. Reconstruction of the earlier castle

Bridgnorth Castle, Shropshire, reconstruction of the stone castle and walled town. The castle is under seige (foreground) from Panpudding Hill

place — chapel and stone buildings. As so often, this castle was built of timber so none of this is visible on the surface. Excavations have produced slight evidence of the traces of foundations of these buildings and a few finds of pottery.

Nearby (bottom left, **99**) is the contemporary Norman church with the typical layout of the period, with three parts — nave, chancel and eastern semicircular apse. All around is the accompanying settlement of peasant houses and farmsteads, some of which have again been found by excavation.

By contrast, figures **100** and **101** show a twelfth- and thirteenth-century stone-built castle at Bridgnorth in Shropshire. This is dramatically sited on a steep-sided spur overlooking the river Severn (beyond the castle and not visible in drawings). All that is left is a substantial part of the tower, but this was blown up in the seventeenth century and now leans at a precarious angle (**102**). The rest of the

Reconstruction of the surviving Tower of Bridgnorth castle

101

castle does not exist now but documents tell us a lot about what was there.

Careful analysis of the tower means that we can understand a lot about how the castle developed (**102**). There was a walled enclosure (rather like an earthen ringwork) with a gatehouse before the tower was begun. The tower was built into the wall by removing a section and may not initially have been built to its full height. Later it was completed, a forebuilding added (shown like an x-ray at the front (**101**)) and a walled enclosure with an entrance incorporated. This almost certainly led into the king's palace buildings, shown (**100**) as a hall and accommodation block.

Beyond the castle defences there was a church and a small Norman defended borough, typical of so many new medieval towns on the Welsh border.

As time went on the need for defence diminished, England being a relatively quiet, well-governed country in relation to many others in Europe in the Middle Ages. Guns and gunpowder, increasingly available from the fourteenth century, also rendered most masonry buildings very vulnerable to attack.

The remains of Bridgnorth castle leaning at an angle after being blown up in the Civil War (seventeenth century). Despite its condition, a sequence of building can be worked out allowing the reconstruction of this tower (left)

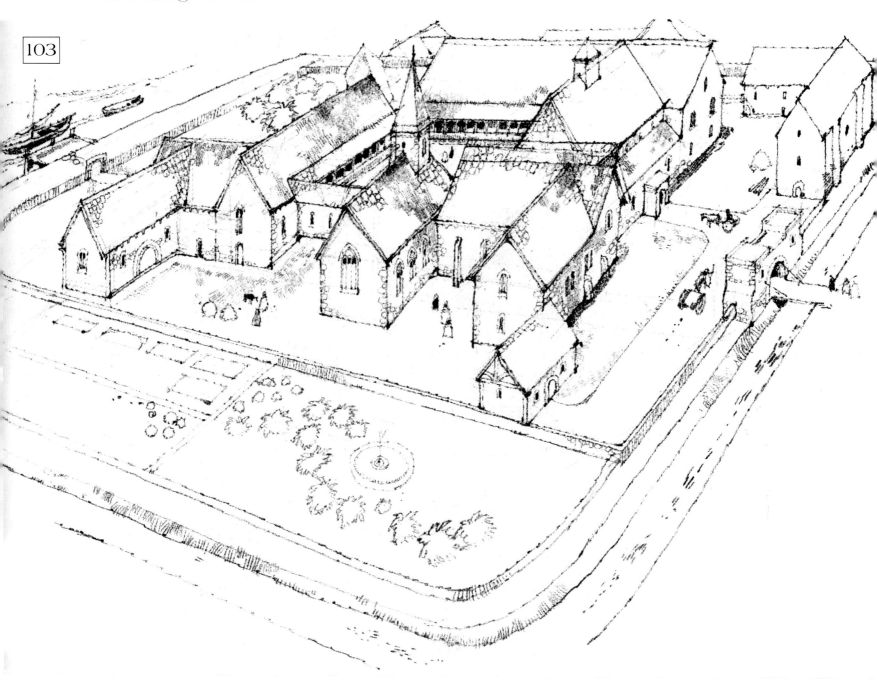

Reconstruction of the royal palace at Richmond, Surrey, c.1390, showing the hall (top centre), domestic buildings and chapel (centre) surrounded by a walled enclosure with gatehouse and gardens, adjacent to the River Thames (left)

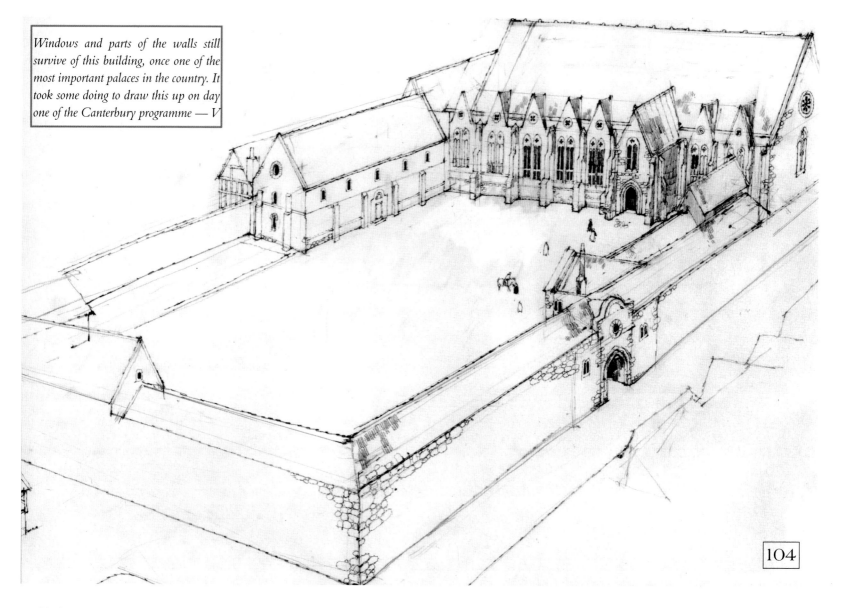

Windows and parts of the walls still survive of this building, once one of the most important palaces in the country. It took some doing to draw this up on day one of the Canterbury programme — V

104

Archbishop's Palace, Canterbury, the great hall and domestic buildings

There had always been (unfortified) palaces belonging to the king, archbishops, bishops and the wealthiest abbots. As in figures **103** and **104**, showing the royal palace at Richmond in *c.*1390 and the Archbishop's palace at Canterbury, these consisted of one or more great open halls with other private apartments, kitchens, service rooms and stores in adjacent buildings. Courts, audiences and official business were carried out in the halls with great pomp and ceremony. Elsewhere there would have been offices, such as an exchequer, to receive the income from manors, lands and estates, and accounting for the enormous expenditure a household like this was involved in.

I drew this inside the solar, which still survives very well, including the fireplace and window. The place had a domestic, peaceful atmosphere, as if it had only been left recently — V

105

Aston Eyre, Shropshire, reconstruction of the interior of the solar (private) wing of the manor house

The gentry lived in smaller versions of these big houses. Figure **105** shows the interior of the private wing (or solar) of a manor house at Aston Eyre in Shropshire. Away from the big draughty open hall with its central fireplace and high-timbered roof space such a room could be comfortable with glazed and shuttered windows, fireplace, painted plastered walls, floor and wall hangings, and pieces of furniture such as beds and chests. In this case there was also an *en suite* garderobe or private loo, which just discharged on to the garden outside. We know from excavations elsewhere that moss and old bits of cloth were used as loo paper (**106**).

106

*Aston Eyre — the medieval loo
at the manor house*

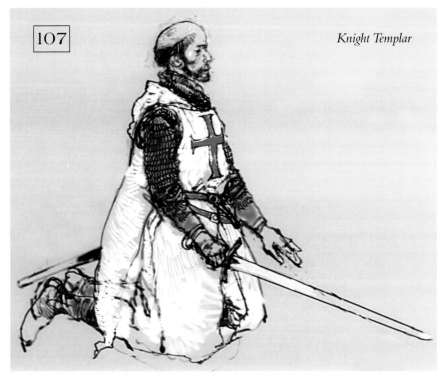

107   *Knight Templar*

(Right) Canterbury — Greyfriars. Only the building in the centre, over the stream, survives. Behind is the church with the domestic buildings attached

(Below) Templecombe, Somerset, the chapel which survived until recently

Medieval England, indeed the whole of Europe, was thickly populated with monastic and religious institutions of one sort and another. There were few towns without an abbey or priory, hospitals and one or more houses of friars. Much of this development belongs to the twelfth and thirteenth centuries — expansion was in effect over by 1300.

Some monasteries were very large and impressive; many of these such as Rievaulx, Tintern and Fountains can be visited today. Most however were much smaller, have not survived so well and we know much less about them. This is particularly true of many of the friaries and hospitals and the establishments belonging to the military orders.

One of the latter has been examined at Templecombe in Somerset. As suggested by the name, this belonged to the Knights Templar, a military order of fighting monks (which sounds like a contradiction in terms) set up around 1100 to defend the holy places in Palestine after the First Crusade.

Each establishment had very few knights (**107**) but money collected and rents would have supported the work of the order overseas. At this site, as at most others in Britain, little remains, although the chapel (**108**) stood until the 1960s.

108

Thetford — Blackfriars. Parts of the church (foreground) remain

Friaries were established when the various groups of friars arrived from the continent in the early 1200s. Dedicated to poverty they did not possess anything, and a site with buildings had to be provided for them, often by the townspeople. They lived by begging and spent their time teaching, preaching and ministering to the sick and poor in an attempt to emulate Christ.

Two examples are shown here — the Greyfriars (Franciscans) at Canterbury and the Black Friars (Dominicans) at Thetford. At Canterbury (**109**) the friars arrived in 1224 and established themselves on an island (bottom right), later moving to a larger, but still restricted, site next door (top

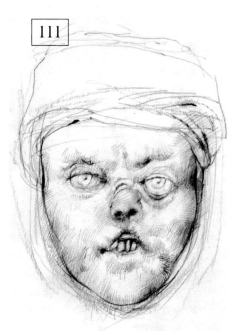

Typical damage to a leper's face. Nose bridge eroded away, nose flattened, eyes hooded, top lip bone destroyed, resulting in a hare lip effect exposing the teeth — V

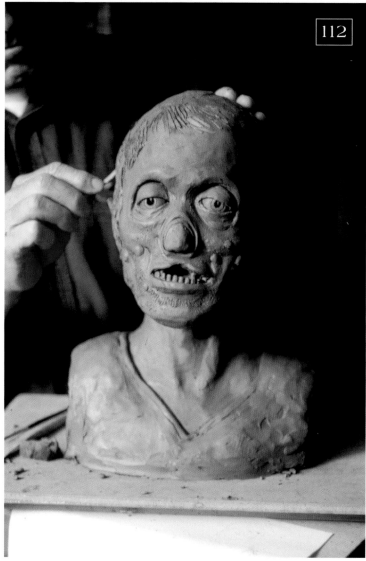

I finally modelled the head on clay, closely advised by Professor Margaret Cox. The end result was frighteningly lifelike. No wonder lepers wore big hats and hoods to hide their faces. They were covered in boils and smelled awful. 'Unclean, unclean...' — V

left). The church there included the large nave used for preaching and a group of service buildings around a space to the south that may never have been a properly developed cloister. Nothing except the building in the centre (of unknown purpose) remains on the site, but much is indicated by geophysical survey and small scale excavations, and it is this information that has been used as the basis for this reconstruction.

At Thetford (**110**) the Black Friars arrived very much later (1335), taking over the old cathedral site (which had also been used for a Cluniac priory) adjacent to the river. Pieces of the church remain built into the school buildings on the site now, and excavation, survey, radar and plan analysis enabled us to reconstruct the church in some detail. It had a central tower over the 'walking place' (a passage across the building), long chancel and nave (also probably for preaching and services for lay people). There were never more than six friars here so the adjacent accommodation with cloister and domestic buildings was generous.

113

Three familiar patients in need of charity! — V

Hospitals were a common and vital feature of medieval towns. Although medical knowledge was scanty and the reasons for disease and sickness were poorly understood, some attempt was made to provide charity and help for the sick and dying. It was believed that attention to the health of the soul was more important than necessarily treating physical signs of disease, so the Church was intimately involved with medicine.

Not all hospitals dealt with the sick; others looked after the old and infirm, travellers and pilgrims, and specialised places looked after lepers, leprosy being a problem until it died out in Britain from the fourteenth century onwards (**111** and **112**).

Usually sisters looked after the inmates with priests and canons on hand to carry out the religious aspects. Patients were often three to a bed and the atmosphere can be imagined as often chilly and very unhealthy.

Figure **113** shows the interior of St Leonards Hospital at York, one of the greatest in the country. Here there was accommodation for over 200 people with a staff of over 50. Readers may recognize the three patients who have just entered (from the left, Tony Robinson, Phil Harding and Mick Aston!).

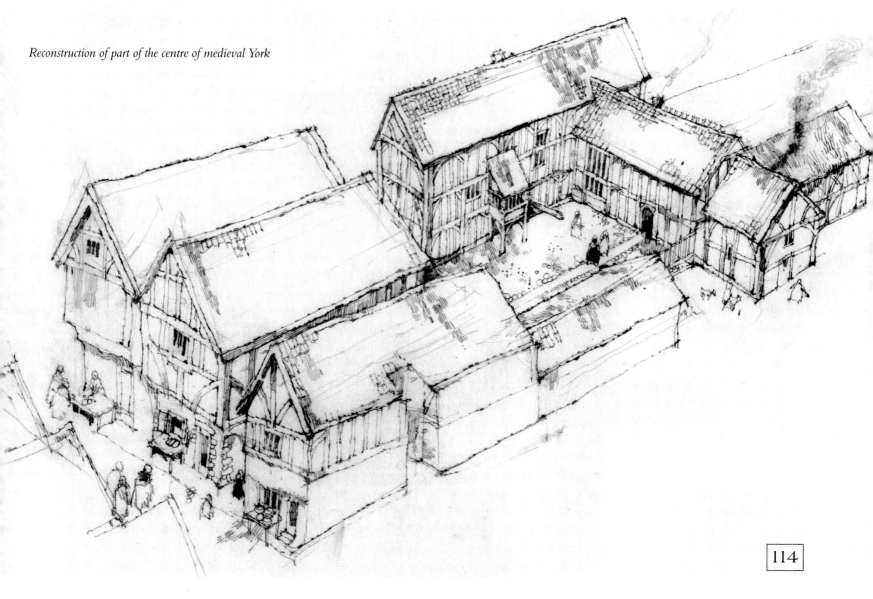

Reconstruction of part of the centre of medieval York

114

Medieval towns were crowded and inhospitable places, where disease spread easily from cess pits and contaminated wells. But even the wealthy lived there, often in fine houses, cheek by jowl with artisans and poor people. Figure **114** shows a reconstruction of part of the centre of medieval York. Buildings along the street frontage (left) have shops and workshops on the ground floor and accommodation behind and above. But in the plots behind is a substantial hall — at right angles to the plot, with a large oriel window lighting the table at the upper end. To the right is the kitchen and service range where food would have been stored and prepared. The large two-storey range provided the high class domestic accommodation. In front was a courtyard approached by an alley off the street; no doubt there were gardens and orchards behind (top right).

115

Plympton, Devon, reconstruction of building with shops on the street frontage, with fine hall behind

A much smaller town but still with a number of late medieval buildings surviving is Plympton in Devon. Figure **115** shows one of them, with entrance and shops at the front under private rooms, and a large hall at the back. Although much of this remains, it has of course been altered and added to over the years. The reconstruction artist can strip all this away, divorce the building from its surroundings and give us part of it cut away to show the roof, making it much easier for us to see the individual elements and how the building functioned.

Jim the potter, appropriately kitted out in contemporary gear turns out wonderful medieval pots! An opportunity to draw live craftsmen in action — V

These towns were the centres of craftwork and industrial activity and they were the places where money and goods were exchanged — the markets and fairs — the shopping centres of the Middle Ages. Some industries were too noisy, smelly or dangerous to be accommodated in towns or they took up too much space. Pottery (**116**) was one of these. It required large quantities of clay and water to make pots in the workshops, and fuel to heat the kilns. There would also have been claypits, drying areas, waste dumps and storage sheds. The reconstruction here is actually a drawing of a modern potter dressed in appropriate clothing who attends re-enactment events. Using only a primitive wheel he makes exquisite jugs, bowls and jars very similar to the remains of those found in excavations. He would have worked indoors or under cover rather than in a makeshift shelter as shown here.

117

Another important medieval industry was tile making, not only producing roofing tiles, but rather more significantly decorated floor tiles for use in churches and monasteries. Figure **117** shows a reconstruction at the recently excavated medieval tile kiln at Tyler's Hill (appropriately named) at Canterbury, above the cathedral and city (which can be seen left in the background). Digging for clay takes place to the left — and there are still traces of the clay pits in the field — while tile-making takes place under the shelter to the right. In the centre the top of the loaded kiln is being finished off, while wood is being fed into the stoke holes at the front.

Such sites, and potteries, generated vast quantities of waste — broken and misfired or misshapen pots which are dumped in any hole or pit which needs filling, or left in piles around the site to the delight of later archaeologists.

Slightly later is the site shown in figures **118** and **119**, recently excavated at Ely. Not far from the cathedral, excavations have shown that late medieval merchants dug channels off the river so that they could bring boats up behind their properties to off-load or take on cargoes.

One of the most important activities here in the late 1500s was potting on a vast scale. Some of these channels were later filled in by vast dumps of waste and broken pottery. One kiln has been excavated (there were probably several) and a reconstruction here shows activities on the site (**119**).

(left) Reconstruction of the medieval tile kiln on Tyler Hill, Canterbury, Kent. All stages of the process of tile-making can be seen here, from digging the clay to firing the tiles (centre)

118

(Right) Ely, Cambridgeshire — the waterside with late medieval boat channels coming off the river

119

The well-preserved sixteenth-century Pottery Kilns at Ely, with our pottery expert working on the wheel in the background — V

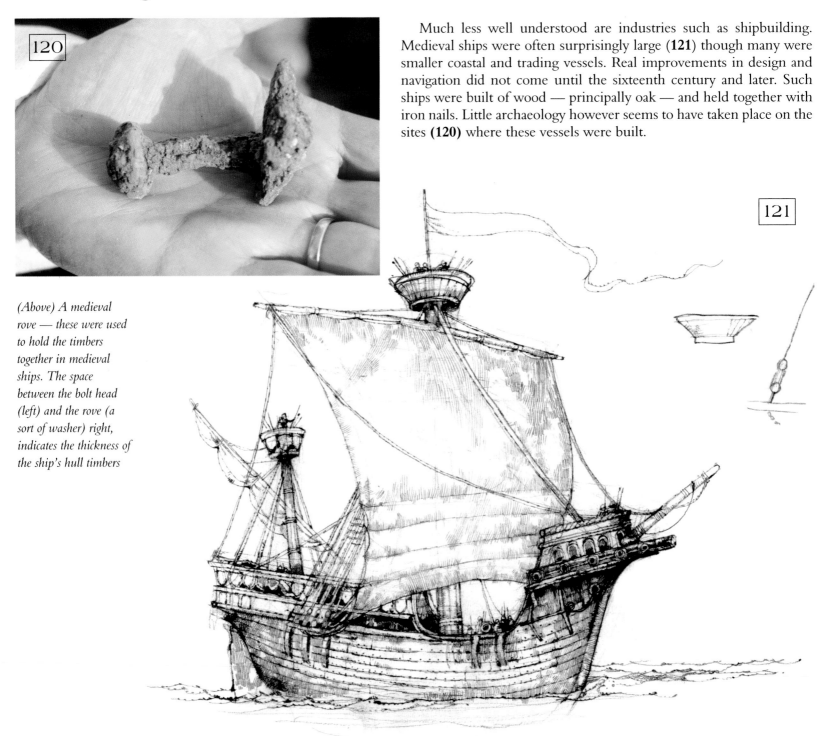

120

Much less well understood are industries such as shipbuilding. Medieval ships were often surprisingly large (**121**) though many were smaller coastal and trading vessels. Real improvements in design and navigation did not come until the sixteenth century and later. Such ships were built of wood — principally oak — and held together with iron nails. Little archaeology however seems to have taken place on the sites (**120**) where these vessels were built.

121

(Above) A medieval rove — these were used to hold the timbers together in medieval ships. The space between the bolt head (left) and the rove (a sort of washer) right, indicates the thickness of the ship's hull timbers

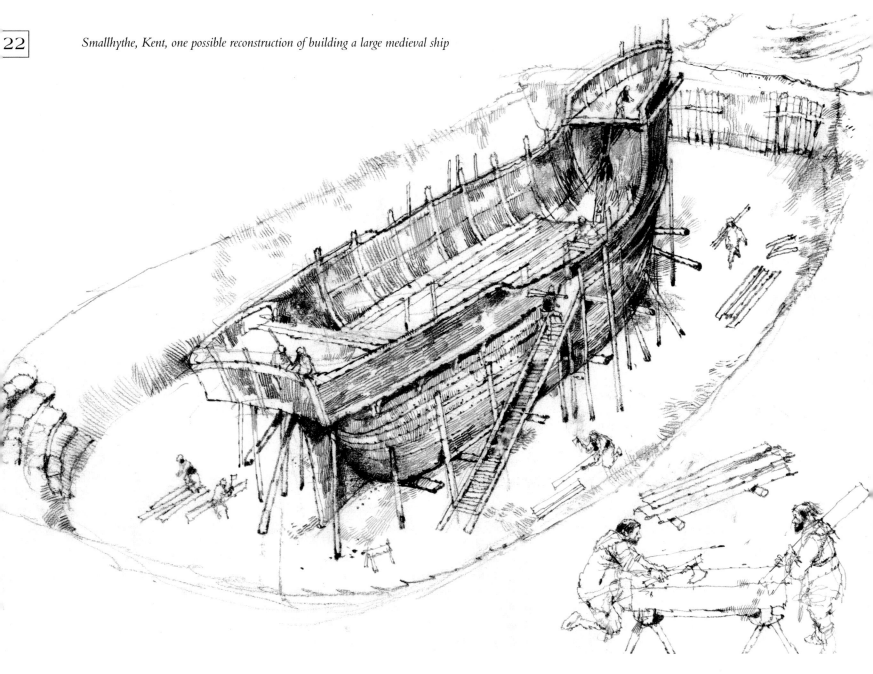

22 *Smallhythe, Kent, one possible reconstruction of building a large medieval ship*

A reconstruction of a medieval shipyard at Smallhythe near Tenterden in Kent is shown in Figures **122** and **123**. We know from documents that large vessels were built here, though now there is no sea or estuary. All the flat area to the right has become silted, has been drained and is now reclaimed as farmland. The site, which was formerly a tidal estuary, is now around 15 miles from the sea.

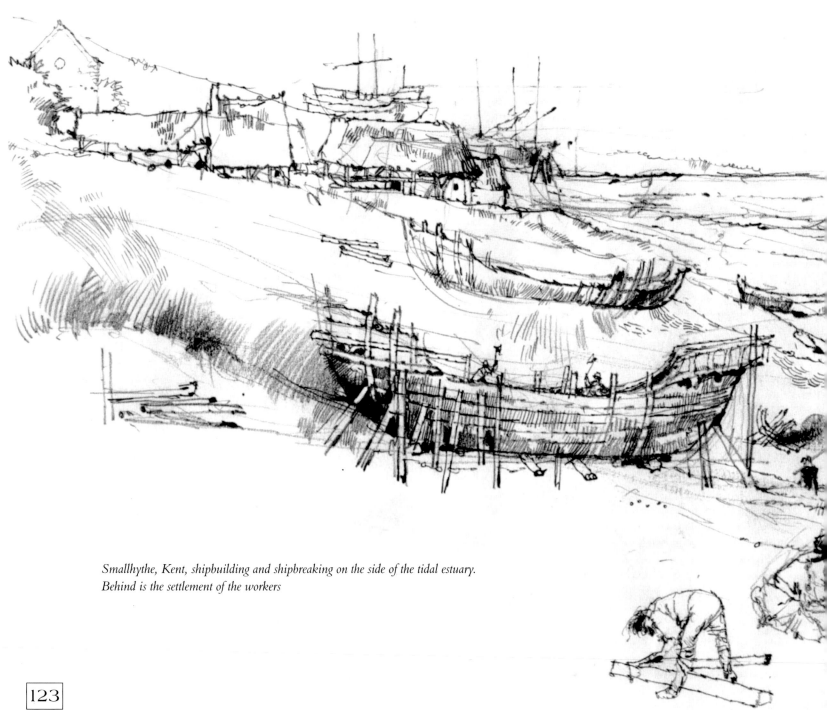

Smallhythe, Kent, shipbuilding and shipbreaking on the side of the tidal estuary.
Behind is the settlement of the workers

123

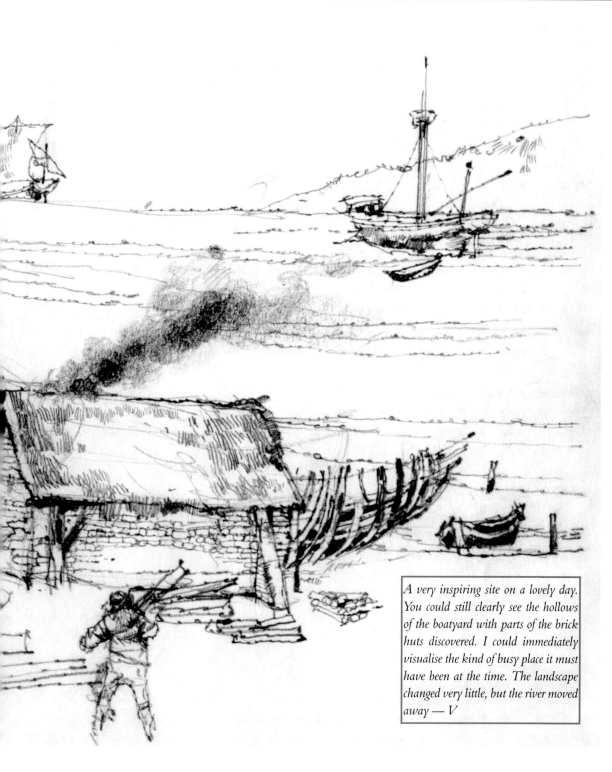

A very inspiring site on a lovely day. You could still clearly see the hollows of the boatyard with parts of the brick huts discovered. I could immediately visualise the kind of busy place it must have been at the time. The landscape changed very little, but the river moved away — V

Excavations at the site suggested that as well as shipbuilding — which probably took place on flat areas by the beach (**122**), rather like the site at Buckler's Hard in Hampshire — there was also ship breaking. Vessels seem to have been dismantled at the end of their working life. No doubt much of the timber was useless and was burned but the ironwork seems to have been collected for recycling. The different *roves* (rather like medieval bolts) found indicate the size of the vessels from the thickness of the former timbers that would have fitted between the pieces of metalwork (**120**). Of course, except for examples of the bits dropped in the mud during construction, these metal parts would go off the site following the launching of the finished vessel. To find them complete, back at the site, suggests dismantling.

The reconstruction shows these activities going on in the foreground. At the rear can be seen the often seasonal and temporary settlement of the workers brought in to carry out the construction and dismantling (**123**).

9 The post-Medieval period

The Middle Ages were well and truly over by the time of the Tudor kings and queens. Not only had the monasteries been dissolved and all their land been redistributed, and new castles (or forts) had been built around the coast, but a greater attention to personal development and privacy had come to the fore. We can see this in new buildings of great houses and palaces and in the new houses (or modifications of old houses) which were being built. From the late fifteenth to the early seventeenth centuries much of the foundation of modern Britain was put in place.

This period was followed in the mid-1600s by the English Civil War (the second after the twelfth-century Anarchy), a particularly vicious and bloody series of campaigns and battles where frequently members of the same family were on opposite sides.

The eighteenth century saw the rise of great houses and landscapes, the result of profit from foreign trade and colonial development but also of increasing industrialisation and improvements in farming technology. The British Empire reached its height in the nineteenth and early twentieth centuries.

This very brief overview of the last 500 years belies the fact that this is a very well-documented (and mapped) period with a vast array of buildings, structures and monuments surviving from it. This, together with the existence of paintings, portraits, diaries, and later on photographs, means that it is a relatively easy period for artists to attempt reconstructions for — often it is more a matter of peopling an existing scene.

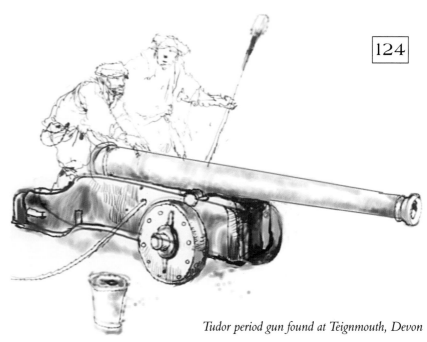

124

However, as with all other periods, there is plenty we don't know about, since as elsewhere, ordinary everyday activities are rarely described or depicted. And, as is common all through the ages, the activities, houses, surroundings and support of the rich and powerful sections of society are always much better studied and represented than anything to do with the lower agricultural or industrial working classes.

Here we provide just a selection of pictures and topics from a very rich period.

Henry VIII, like other Tudor monarchs, was concerned about the security and defence of England. He initiated a series of forts (Deal, Walmer, Sandown and so on) around the South Coast as an anti-invasion measure (a trend that was 1500 years

Tudor period gun found at Teignmouth, Devon

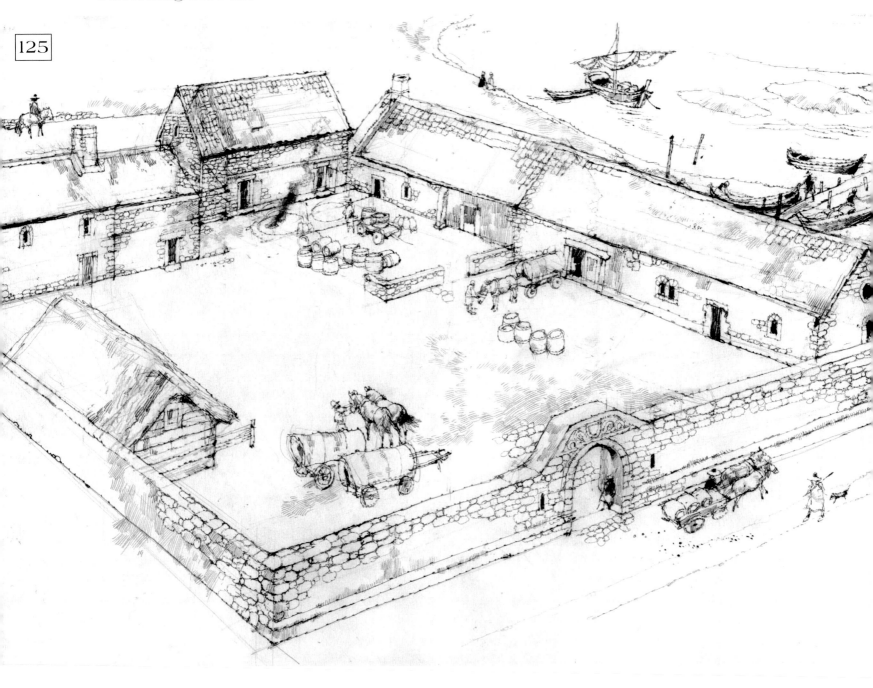

Victualling yard at Holy Island, Northumberland

old by then and which was to continue to develop for another 400 years). As well as these forts there were naval installations and supply bases.

Figure **125** shows a recently examined site on Holy Island, best known for its early monastery, Lindisfarne, on the Northumberland coast. It is clear that the sea used to form a great embayment by the Heugh and the castle and that this provided a safe sheltered anchorage on this rough coast (top right). The governor's house was off the picture to the left with this yard of supply buildings adjacent to it.

The yard included a brewery (top centre) where ale was made for the garrison and visiting ships. No doubt a variety of other trades and activities were carried out here to victual the ships.

Tudor monarchs were right to be concerned about coastal defence as was eventually seen with the Spanish Armada of 1588. This might well have resulted in an invasion and take over by Catholic

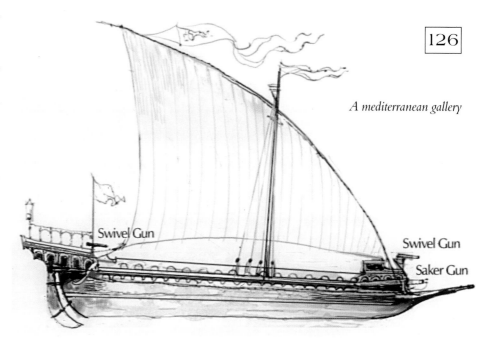

126

A mediterranean gallery

Swivel Gun

Swivel Gun

Saker Gun

127 *Mick doing town plan analysis*

Spain of Elizabeth I's newly Protestant England.

When several guns were raised from a wreck off Teignmouth in Devon (**124**) it was assumed they were from an Armada wreck. However further examinations showed that this was not the case but that the ship was almost certainly a Mediterranean galley type of vessel propelled by oars as well as sails and armed with several swivel guns as well as the larger saker gun (**126**).

What was such a vessel doing off the English coast and why Teignmouth in particular? It was clearly at that time engaged in maritime trade and probably went down in a storm. The coast of Britain is littered with wrecks of many types of vessels of all periods.

Teignmouth itself was a port, though today it is a holiday and retirement town and a centre for yachting. A different type of artistic reconstruction is needed to demonstrate this. Town plan analysis (**127**), using existing maps and what is known from old maps and documents, enables us to suggest what such places looked like in earlier times and therefore the context of the wreck site of our galley. Figures **128**, **129** and **130** show three hypothetical stages in the development of the town and coast at Teignmouth. Because estuaries change, become eroded or

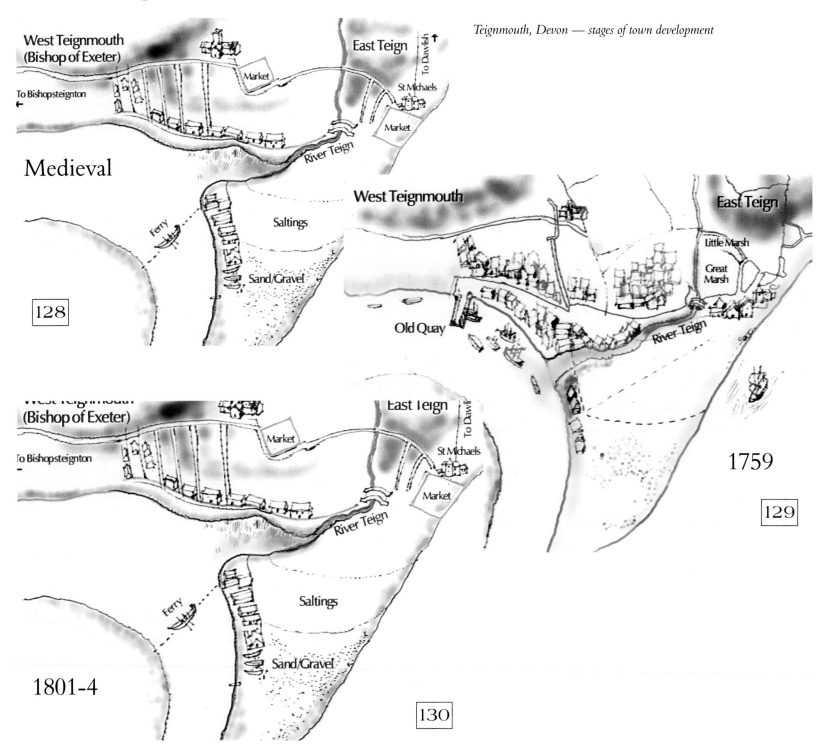

Teignmouth, Devon — stages of town development

West Teignmouth
(Bishop of Exeter)

To Bishopsteignton

Market

East Teign

To Dawlish

St Michaels

Market

River Teign

Medieval

Ferry

Saltings

Sand/Gravel

128

West Teignmouth

East Teign

Little Marsh

Great Marsh

Old Quay

River Teign

1759

129

West Teignmouth
(Bishop of Exeter)

To Bishopsteignton

Market

East Teign

To Dawlish

St Michaels

Market

River Teign

1801-4

Ferry

Saltings

Sand/Gravel

130

A great Tudor palace at Rycote near Oxford. The large drawing took two days and was never quite finished. Hardly anything of the house survives, but we had one of two very old prints of what it looked like. Reconstructing the gardens was another problem, and after much argument we decided that this version may be too late for the period — V

Rycote, Oxfordshire — reconstruction of the gardens

clogged up with silt, sand bars move with deposition of sand, gravel and silt, and erosion by the sea during storms, such plans can only ever be conjectural. In this case the reconstruction artist's maps suggest the site of the medieval and later port as part of the early development of Teignmouth which shows us why the foreign trading vessel should have been found here.

The increasing wealth, general security and attention to good living and leisure at the upper end of the social scale was manifested in the construction of large country houses (one might almost call them palaces) from the Tudor period onwards. Figure **131** shows one of these at Rycote in Oxfordshire. Often these were built in the relatively new material — brick, with stone quoins and window and door frames. As well as halls and private rooms, there were apartments for visitors and a long gallery for indoor recreation.

Surrounding these houses, **132** shows part of a formal garden with squared off flower beds, gravel paths and focal fountains, trees and sundials. There was much expansion and development of gardens at this time, a trend that had begun in the Middle Ages. Beyond the formal gardens and all around the house there would invariably be a park with deer and domestic animals grazing as well as stands of woodland.

This relatively peaceful period was interrupted by the English Civil Wars. Supporters of the king (Cavaliers) and of parliament (Roundheads) fought it out in pitched battles, which many of us remember from history lessons — Edgehill, Naseby — and rather more common small-scale skirmishes. In our minds, and from artists 'reconstructions, we tend to think of the two sides as very different in appearances with cavaliers dressed in finery with their long hair and roundheads in uniforms with armour — the reality was that each side dressed, behaved and was similarly equipped and that it was in fact very difficult to tell whose side anyone was on in the thick of a fight (**134**).

At Basing House, near Basingstoke in Hampshire, there was a particularly vicious skirmish between the royalists in the castle and the attacking parliamentarians (**133 & 135**). Here a Norman castle of a ring work and several baileys had been developed as a major brick-built residence for the Paulet family. An older house (or palace) had been replaced by a newer one. The gatehouse was stormed as we see here, a lot of lead shot was fired and bloody hand-to-hand fighting took place.

The castle site had in fact been surrounded by siegeworks built of timber and turf with ditches. Lines of banks linked up several gun platforms on which cannon could be mounted to fire at the Basing House buildings (**136**). Such earthen defences, on both sides were quick to build, and demolish, and provided the best means of absorbing cannon fire. The guns themselves could be moved and manoeuvred into the best positions for attack. Each gun needed a crew, and as we see here gunpowder would need to be stored nearby and some temporary accommodation provided when the crew was not actually in action. The ammunition (cannonballs) could as easily be made of stone as iron or lead.

133

133

Of all the site reconstructions that I have worked on, the siege of Basing House was one of the most complex. From burnt fragments, pieces of discoloured glass and lead pistol balls, we gradually pieced together a ferocious attack on one of the towers that we were digging at. The door was blocked and barricaded up with rubble, and the roundheads had to attack the first floor. The roof was set alight and the defenders poured fire from the windows.

The roundhead cavalry used siege ladders to get at them at great cost to themselves. Once the tower was taken, Basing House fell to the Parliamentarians — V

A Civil War skirmish — Roundhead (Parliamentarian) on the left, Cavalier (Royalist) on the right slogging it out! A lot of this would have taken place during a siege. It gave me a chance to indulge my favourite subject, horses — V

134

135

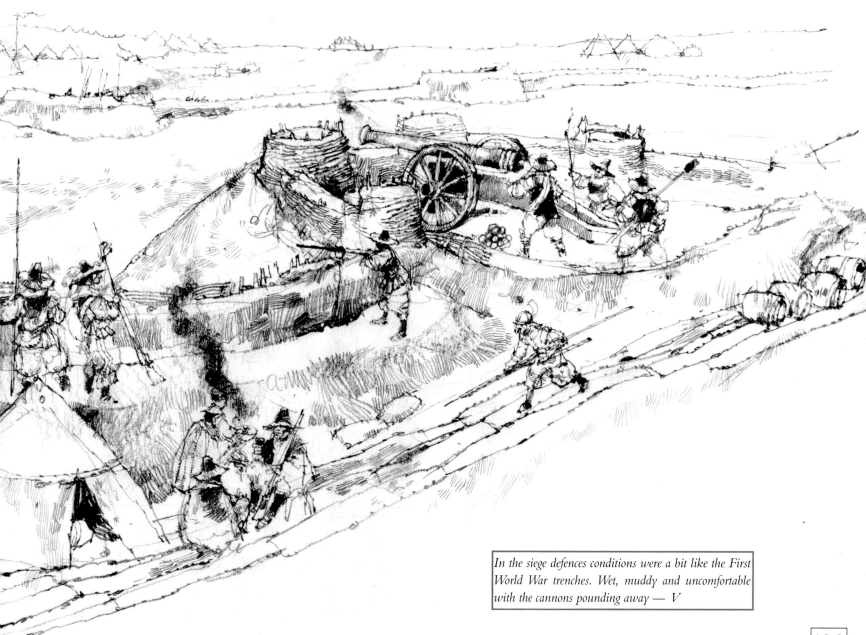

In the siege defences conditions were a bit like the First World War trenches. Wet, muddy and uncomfortable with the cannons pounding away — V

136

8 The recent past

While it is clear that there was increasing industrial activity in the seventeenth century, we think of the industrial revolution as taking place in the eighteenth century. From the 1600s there is certainly a vast increase in the material equipment — pottery, metal work and so on — evident from the archaeology of any site excavated from that period onwards.

In the 1700s however, a fundamental change occurred. Objects that had been individually made in craft workshops as single items in the past were henceforth made to a uniform design on a factory scale. Such replication in moulds, whether it was of coins, metal items or pottery, meant that far more could be produced and we see the result in the vast quantities of post-medieval finds from most archaeological excavations of the period. Such production consumed far more raw materials (and produced more waste products) and needed an adequate transport system to supply these and to take away the finished products. The canal system and then railways were developed to supplement and replace the inadequate road network, which had only been partially improved by Turnpike Trusts upgrading various toll roads. Concentrations of workers around the factories produced new settlements and suburbs, reinforcing the slum conditions in which the rural and urban working classes lived in the eighteenth and nineteenth centuries.

All this activity demanded the consumption of a lot more energy. Water power (and to a much lesser extent wind power) had been the only form of energy other than the muscles of people and animals up to the development of steam engines in the eighteenth century. The water for these was heated by the use of coal, which came to replace charcoal, the pre-industrial fuel, as the main source of energy.

137

The viaduct at Blaenavon — it was covered over and had houses in the arches underneath

(Far left) Air view of blast furnaces at Blaenaron

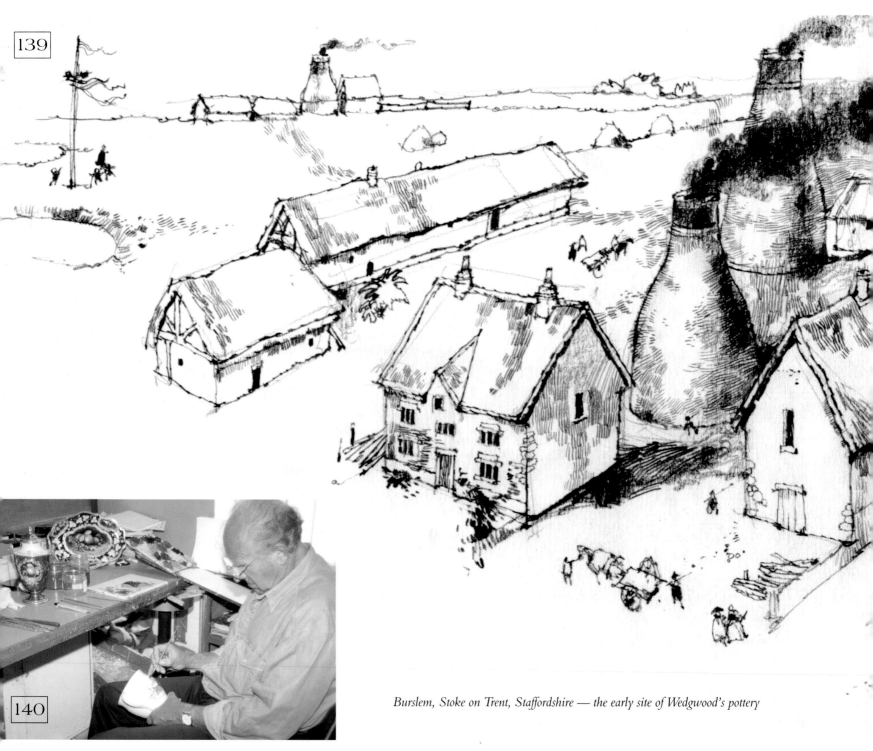

139

140

Burslem, Stoke on Trent, Staffordshire — the early site of Wedgwood's pottery

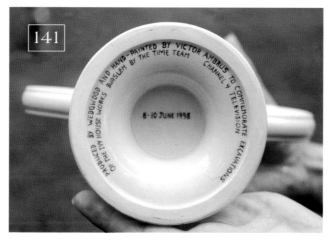

141

The ultimate challenge. I was asked to decorate a Wedgwood vase with a painting of the first pottery works. The Wedgwood painters said it could not be done in a day. I did it between 10am and 4.30pm, and nearly went blind over it!

Here is the end product. I was asked to join the Wedgwood painters; good holiday terms and pension were mentioned. I will keep it in mind! — V

142

One of many areas involved in this frenetic activity was South Wales. Here the existence of coal, limestone and iron ore on a large scale provided the basis for an extensive iron-working industry. At Blaenavon the blast furnaces can still be seen on a Cadw (Welsh Historic Monuments) managed site (**137**), and nearby are the coal and iron mines which supplied the raw materials. A rare structure, a viaduct with houses beneath (**138**), stood in this area. Trucks full of iron ore were pushed or pulled along trackways to the furnaces across the viaduct. It was a big undertaking to construct this and it indicates the scale of activities. Later on the valley was infilled with mining waste and then the whole site covered in twentieth-century landfill. But as far as can be seen this extraordinary structure must still survive buried in waste in the valley.

By contrast is the site shown in figure **139** which shows a reconstruction of the early pottery factory of Wedgwood at Burslem in Stoke-on-Trent. Here Josiah Wedgwood experimented with early moulded whiteware pottery before moving on to the more famous factory at Etruria. The reconstruction shows two bottle-shaped buildings that cover the pottery kilns where the pots were fired. Around this are the yards where the clay was prepared, vessels made and dried, and glazing took place. The owner's house is at the front. In the background other kilns, potteries and houses can be seen with areas of common and wasteland where the workers would have grazed a few animals. On the far left Victor is shown decorating a modern pot made to commemorate *Time Team's* visit in 1998. A reconstruction scene was applied and the pot is now in the ceramic exhibition centre at Burslem.

All of this was to change in the nineteenth century as this and other industries expanded at an enormous rate. New factories were built and extensive areas of housing developed.

In our post-industrial age much of this activity and the landscapes that go with it are redundant and are being demolished and reclaimed for other purposes. The role of the reconstruction artist is thus as vital for this later period as it is for the earlier ones. Without their skill many people in future will not be able to envisage what the twentieth century replaced of this earlier activity.

Endpiece (Victor)

After Mick Aston's chronologically set out and scholarly-explained main section, I present a miscellany of drawings of other sites and subjects that I have found very interesting. They range from the Welsh 'Celtic Spring' site of a wonderful setting and no archaeology, to details of Roman life and death at Hadrian's Wall and some other glorious landscapes such as Cheddar Gorge, the Island of Nevis and Holy Island.

143

They bring back memories of sun-baked beaches in the West Indies, horizontal rain in the Scottish Islands and torrential downpours when I was drawing the cremation scene at Birdoswald, Cumbria. Never a dull moment for an illustrator, you may be asked to reconstruct the town and castle of Bridgeworth in two days, or to draw Tony Robinson and Mick Aston in a Roman bathhouse in ten minutes flat!

Over the past few years I have been privileged to work side-by-side with the cream of this country's archaeologists. I meet the experts on pathology, buildings, castles, coins, ceramics, Roman life, medieval times, manuscripts and many other aspects of archaeology. I have learned a lot from them, and I am still learning. Prior to my involvement with

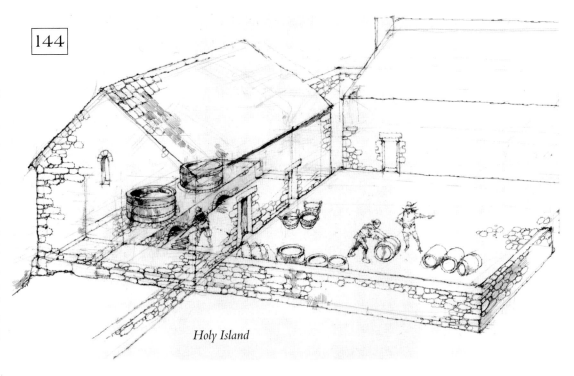

144

Holy Island

145

Time Team I had illustrated many historical books including reconstructions of buildings and events but I had never been involved in the nitty-gritty and 'mud' of archaeology — a real 'dig' on site and discovering history as it is uncovered step-by-step.

Nearly all the drawings that you see here, including the colour illustrations, were produced on site in a short period: three days. They were mostly produced in pencil, because they were altered many, many times until we finally agreed on the most probable version.

The war on the sea. Navel victories were crucial during the Napoleonic wars. Here a boarding party setting out to capture a ship. — V

A drawing that I did near the Brecon Beacons in south Wales. It was a wonderful landscape, archaeology in a magnificent setting. Unfortunately all of the 'standing stones', 'celtic springs', and 'towers' turned out to be phoney!
— V

146

147

Occasionally you are asked to reconstruct a real handful, such as a stage coach. This is the Bristol to London Royal Mail. I enjoyed drawing the horses and top hats — V

148

Postman/messenger in the early seventeenth century, just before the Civil War. These complex and colourful costumes are a real treat to paint compared with Roman togas or Saxon clothing — V

The mobs of the French Revolution also make exciting subjects. I went to Paris to research the costumes, hair styles and weapons — V

149

I am very grateful to Tim Taylor, the Producer, and Mick Aston, Team Leader, for plucking me from my sheltered life of illustrating books into the extraordinary experience of working with the one big happy family called the *Time Team*, and you could not meet nicer people. During my work on the programmes I have also seen some magnificent reconstructions produced by other illustrators (particularly for English Heritage), drawn in colour and in great detail. The inheritance of Alan Sorrel lives on and is flourishing. In a world of pickled cows in the Tate, drawing still matters to illustrators, because people won't settle for anything less. We have these drawings to help describe, explain and bring alive the past, so that we can all share in it.

Index

Ambrus and Aston index
(Numbers in bold = the page number for the illustration)